BRASS TACKS TIPS FOR BUSINESS OWNERS

Brass Tacks Tips for Business Owners

Nitty-gritty know-how for improving
personal performance and building
value in your company

Answers to the most common questions
challenging business owners, entrepreneurs
and innovative managers

Dr. Paul A. Willax

To Robin & Chris —
with great appreciation
for your encouragement
and friendship!

paul

Writers Club Press
San Jose New York Lincoln Shanghai

Brass Tacks Tips for Business Owners
Nitty-gritty know-how for improving personal performance and building
value in your company

All Rights Reserved © 2002 by Paul A. Willax

Writers Club Press
an imprint of iUniverse, Inc.

For information address:
iUniverse, Inc.
5220 S. 16th St., Suite 200
Lincoln, NE 68512
www.iuniverse.com

Brass Tacks, BrainFood and *MetaManagement* are Registered Trademarks of Paul A. Willax and the Center for Business Ownership Inc.
The author is providing this material for general information purposes only and is not engaged in providing legal, accounting, insurance, or investment advice or counsel. If expert assistance is required, the services of a qualified professional should be sought. While reasonable care has been taken in the preparation of this content, the author and the publisher assume no liability for actions taken by inndividuals using this material.

ISBN: 0-595-21792-3

Printed in the United States of America

To Shelley, Jen and Jon,
my best supporters,
who can be counted on for the kind of
inspiration, aggravation and adulation
that an old scrivener needs to pound it out.

A special thank you to Shelley, a proofreader
extraordinaire.

Contents

PREFACE

In the following pages, owners of small and mid-size businesses will find some important **Brass Tacks®** **Tips** for improving their performance as entrepreneurs and enhancing the value of their enterprises. The fifty articles offered in the following pages constitute my responses to the questions most frequently directed to me for consideration in my syndicated newspaper columns. These queries have come to me over the years via snail mail, e-mail, fax, telephone and shouting from the factory-tops.

My replies have been published in *Brass Tacks®* and *Minding Everybody's Business®* columns that have appeared in newspapers and magazines, and on the Internet, radio, television, and lavatory walls across the country. However, this is the first time that the responses to those noteworthy queries have been compiled and boldly presented between two classy, color covers.

The *pearls of wisdom* offered herein are a product of my half-century of experience as a business owner, entrepreneur and journalist and are based on my personal exposure to many successful—and a few not so successful—real-life entrepreneurs.

The common thread: *Valuable, need-to-know "stuff" that can make a critical top and bottom line difference to an ambitious venturer.* Included is the kind of practical, *been there, done that* advice that you won't get from most publications, seminars or business school curricula. It's information, insight and inspiration you can put to use, pronto.

Whether your mission du jour involves mastering a threatening challenge or exploiting a once-in-a-lifetime opportunity, you'll find a lot of sage help—and some solace—in the following pages.

INTRODUCTION

Based on the premise that "experience is the best teacher," this collection of articles is compiled and formatted in a manner that will conserve your time while providing you with immediately-actionable ideas.

These nutritious servings **of *Brass Tacks*® *Tips*** have been cooked up to serve primarily owners of small and mid-size businesses, but managers and corporate executives will find many valuable insights as well.

The enclosed articles are responses to the most frequently-voiced concerns of entrepreneurial venturers who are blazing trails in today's competitive marketplaces. Since many of the specific questions that have been directed my way over the past few years are similar in nature, I've reformulated gaggles of related queries into fifty salient questions that mirror the interests of today's ambitious business owners and entrepreneurs.

I am ever amazed at the similarity of needs and interests evidenced by entrepreneurial movers and shakers. Year after year, the same types of questions are asked and concerns voiced. Certainly, as time changes, the thrust, focus or details of each inquiry change, but the same types of basic issues emerge with consistency. Many of these issues have endured since the beginning of entrepreneurial time. But, thanks to experience, new technology and snowballing knowledge, the answers change as time passes. The enclosed articles reflect these time-worn challenges but provide *contemporary* observations, insights and answers in response.

Importantly, if you don't find the answer here and aren't willing to wait for the next edition, simply visit **http://www.thebrasstacks.com/** to log in your question or express your concern.

Finally, I hope you appreciate that you are confronted with a real bargain. Your author has labored to include, in addition to his gems of hard-gained wisdom, the observations and admonitions of some other sages who've evidenced a knack for saying things better—and certainly more succinctly—than I do. These appear at the top of each article, free of charge.

BUILD A WINNING MODEL

The whole of science is nothing more than a refinement of everyday thinking.

—Albert Einstein, Physicist

Any seamstress will tell you that a pattern is essential to a fashion that sells.

Q. I'm reading more and more about the importance of having a good "business model." I am in the process of adding a new product line, and I'm not sure what a "model" is or whether I even need one. Can you clarify this for me?

A. Simply stated, a "business model" is your description of the way you intend to arrange and use tangible and intangible resources to provide your existing or prospective customers with unique value. You have to focus on a value that they will want both now and in the future—one that they'll be willing to pay the "right" price for. By right price, I mean a price that will afford your firm an operating margin (the difference between the selling price and what a product or service costs) that will fund a "bottom line" profit. In essence, a model is a personal depiction of your basic premise for creating initial revenue and ultimate profit.

Furthermore, a model is a template for action that will profitably configure your firm's resources to a market need within a prescribed time frame. Few ventures can be profitable and cash-positive from their inception. Time is required to "prime the corporate pump," to sell, and to collect. Therefore, an undertaking's break-even point must be achievable with a time period in which these operations can be sustained with available cash.

Sounds pretty simple and straightforward. Anybody who's ever had a paper route should intuitively understand the relevance of a business model. But you'd be surprised how many entrepreneurial "wannabe's"—especially in today's high-tech, anything's-possible environment—overlook this fundamental need for a perception of how everything is going to come together in a way that justifies the required investment of resources.

Because entrepreneurs are, by nature, eager, impatient, optimistic and supremely self-confident creatures, they are often inclined to a "ready, fire, aim" approach when it comes to chasing their dream du jour. Since the concept of a "model' is so simple, they tend to underestimate its importance and profound long-term implications. As a consequence, they frequently jump to implementation before their dreams and desires are translated into a conceptual prototype that can be adequately pre-tested.

The folly of this oversight is reflected today in the tragic experiences of the many dot-com swashbucklers who swaggered, with only hype and hope, into ventures that were ill conceived and unsustainable. Moreover, since they lacked a sound business archetype at the commencement of their capers, they didn't have the perspective and practical foundation necessary to successfully re-forge their undertakings once their junkets were underway and floundering.

To be sure, there'd be many more happy faces in Silicon Valley today if every venturer had just paused to consider:

The top line: Every worthwhile business concept must be able to demonstrate that there is—or, given feasible and affordable marketing efforts, that there will soon be—a sufficient, continuing stream of revenue to energize it. The real magic worked by entrepreneurs involves the creation of "top lines" for their enterprises. They do that by finding consumers who will give them money—now and again and again in the foreseeable future—for the values they have created or cobbled together.

By examining a detailed depiction (i.e. model) of your intentions prior to acting, you'll be forced to answer some important questions, thus minimizing the risk of your undertaking. To wit: **Are you really, absolutely, positively, definitely sure that you are offering such unique value that a prospective customer will readily see it as a "solution" for which he is willing to pay your price in the belief that it cannot be obtained on more favorable terms or in a better configuration from another source?**

Re-read this question three times before moving on. Why are you so sure? Will you be able to maintain this uniqueness and desirability—and sales level—in the face of competitive incursions or changing consumer tastes and requirements? Do you know who your first twenty-five customers are—by name—and have you talked to them personally about their perceptions of the value you propose to offer? What will be required to keep these customers buying from you over and over and over? Keep in mind that without an ever-present "top line," you have no business!

The margin: Can you charge a price that makes sense? Will your pricing afford you a continuing, positive spread between what you charge and what it costs to produce the goods or service you are selling? Will this spread be sufficient to cover selling and administrative costs? Remember, a low-ball introductory price strategy generally results in continuing low margin levels. If relatively low pricing is essential as an opening gambit, are you sure that you will be able to adjust pricing realistically down the line? How soon? Do you have enough cash in hand to fund your deficits in the interim? For how long?

The in-between lines: There are a lot of hungry "mouths" to feed on the journey from the top line to the bottom line. For example, the costs associated with getting and keeping good sales people and technology mavens can be enormous, especially if you are taking them on a bumpy journey. You also have to finance the tangible and intangible assets that are needed to devise and deliver value. Will your prospective customers pay you quickly enough to cover these costs? Have you produced a monthly cash flow projection that succeeds in matching real inflows with real outflows? Will you be able to fund all cash flow deficits without taking your surplus cash to zero??

The bottom line: Will you be able to juggle all the above-mentioned "lines" in a way that eventually—and on a regular basis—produces more cash than you require to sustain and grow the business? Volumes and timing are the keys. Can you generate enough cash flow soon enough—and long enough—to make this venture worth the candle?

If you come up with more than one unanswerable question, immeasurable gap, incalculable estimate, or instance of wishful thinking, go back directly to the drawing board and DO NOT PASS GO. According to ol' uncle Ollie, when it comes to business, forget the eager heart and go with the calculating mind. "It's definitely not better to have loved (your idea) and lost (your money), than to have never loved at all."

MANAGE ENTREPRENEURIALLY

Entrepreneurship is behavior. Anybody can learn behavior.
—Peter Drucker, Educator and Author

The entrepreneur has become the toast of the town. Still, many folks remain confused about the nature and role of the entrepreneur.

Q. I just inherited a sizeable business from my dad. Previously, I enjoyed a successful career as a corporate manager. I'm looking forward to being a real entrepreneur but I recently read an article by Bill Gates in which he claims that the only true definition of an entrepreneur is "one who starts a business." Does this mean that a guy like me will forever be a fish out of water?

A. While Bill will probably go down in history as one of the most successful entrepreneurs who ever lived, I can't agree with his narrow definition of an entrepreneur. In the article you've cited, Mr. Gates embraces the classic definition which holds that an entrepreneur is "somebody who has *started* his or her own company." He decries the fact that the title has become almost meaningless since "it has grown to have many positive connotations with little specificity."

Gates focuses exclusively on the economic function of an entrepreneur and not on his or her innovative behavior, the real key to success in business. We should keep in mind that, throughout history, the term "entrepreneurship" referred to a type of behavior as well as to an economic role played. Of French origin, the word is derived from "entre prend," words that signify "between-taking," the activities by which an entrepreneur seizes a position between resources and opportunities and, because of his or her unique behavior, makes something positive happen.

One of the first uses of the word was in the late 1700's by Jean Baptiste Say, an economist who is credited with developing the concept of entrepreneurship. He described an entrepreneur in terms of behavior. "He is called upon," said Say, "to estimate, with tolerable accuracy, the importance of a specific product, the probable amount of demand, and the means of production; sometimes to employ a great number of hands; again to buy or order raw materials, to combine the workers, find consumers, to exercise a spirit of order and economy. In the course of such operations, there are obstacles to be surmounted, anxieties to be overcome, misfortunes to be repaired, and expedients to be devised." Save but for the first word, this is an accurate definition today.

During the 19th century, the "ability to take calculated risks" was added to the definition. By mid-twentieth century, the importance of innovative talent—the ability to find and profitably introduce new and better products, services and processes—was recognized and included in the entrepreneur's "job description."

At no time, however, was it concluded that these important business-building tasks could be performed only by someone who is starting a new enterprise.

Today, these are critical tasks in every business firm, from the corner used car lot to General Motors. Companies of every stripe—new, old, emerging, established—all depend upon entrepreneurial behavior to achieve survival, success and sustainability.

Indeed, innovative talent has become the hallmark of the entrepreneur. Given the current pace of change, especially in market preferences, technology and competition, it has become incumbent upon every manager to constantly re-create his or her enterprise in order to keep it vital and relevant. The history of every successful enterprise is marked by a continuum of "start-over points" at which the venture was "recast" in form or function to master the challenges and opportunities of the day.

As a consequence, business owners should never outgrow their entrepreneurial beginnings, and managers must learn how to perpetually perform as entrepreneurs. Each must be able to continuously identify opportunity, organize talents, assume risks and make ready-decisions to create value. Because of such entrepreneurial innovation, a firm will be ever-able to exploit new, different, and better techniques, processes, and product/service configurations.

According to management guru Peter Drucker, the most important distinguishing characteristic of the entrepreneur is his or her ability to innovate. He says: "Innovation is the means by which entrepreneurs exploit change as an opportunity for a different business." Once again, there is no suggestion that this type of behavior is limited to people who are devoted to creating new businesses from scratch.

Notwithstanding the above, we probably do a disservice to the true entrepreneur by attaching the "e" appellation to everyone who owns a business. For example, the proprietor of a pizzeria is not necessarily an entrepreneur. An entrepreneur, by definition, is innovative, a change agent who "creatively destroys" the status quo in a quest for new and better ways to satisfy consumers and create value. (Noted economist Joseph Schumpeter believed that "creative destruction" of the old ways of operating within a firm was necessary at precisely the point at which management starts enjoying the comfort, predictability and stability of the status quo.) The true entrepreneurial innovator was the individual who first perceived the potential domestic demand for the savory "pies" that American GI's discovered in Italy during World War Two. Tom Monaghan, the founder of Domino's Pizza who pioneered rapid, reliable home delivery, is also an entrepreneur in the true sense of the word. So will be the first person to produce a diet pizza.

To be sure, an entrepreneurial personality is needed to start a business. But this kind of behavior is also essential in an established company that fights to keep its competitive edge.

Brass Tacks Tip: Bill Gates would be in big trouble if he were the only entrepreneur working at Microsoft today.

The art of entrepreneurship can be profitably applied in established companies as well as in small, start-up ventures. Every "established" firm has to be perpetually "re-started" by a foresightful leader in order to maintain its relevance and vitality. And this requires the innovativeness and industriousness of an entrepreneur who can also master management skills.

I call this combination of management ability and entrepreneurial savvy *MetaManagement.* The term "meta" means beyond, and *MetaManagement* refers to management behaviors that go beyond mere administration. However, in order for your firm to benefit from this entrepreneurial power, its key leaders must truly feel like entrepreneurs, and this requires a work environment in which:

• There is a visionary, strategic plan for the company and a customized, agreed-upon mission contract with each leader.

• Employees enjoy the authority to experiment, test, and make changes.

• Team members are rewarded, like owners, either through "virtual" ownership techniques (e.g. profit-sharing) or actual equity-sharing programs featuring things like stock options, ESOP's or share awards. A "piece of the action" is essential for a true entrepreneur.

• There are opportunities to try new approaches to product development, marketing or production and processing.

• There is easy access to decision-makers within the firm and to all of the firm's customer constituencies.

• There is a tolerance for unique behavior and failure.

• Everyone is recognized for his or her individual performance. *MetaManagers* need "stage time" and applause to keep the level of confidence and self-esteem that is necessary for successful entrepreneurial behavior.

• The presiding CEO is a team leader who is able to articulate a vision, coach, take risks and share the spoils.

It is up to a firm's CEO—its *Chief Entrepreneurial Officer*—to provide an environment that will allow an innovative spirit to prevail and *MetaManagers* to flourish. As ol' uncle Ollie said: "Managers do things right, but *MetaManagers* do the right things."

INNOVATE TO ADVANCE

The creation of something new is not accomplished by the intellect but by the 'play instinct' acting from inner necessity. The creative mind plays with the objects it loves.

—Carl Jung, Psychologist and Psychiatrist

It has been said that "ideas are a dime a dozen." But, still, some people fear that they won't be able to find a good idea at any price.

Q. I am in a very mature business with limited future demand for our product. I want my firm to continue to prosper by moving in a new direction, but I worry that all of the good ideas are taken and, since I'm not a genius inventor, I'll never reach this goal. What's left to invent?

A. Not to worry. There's opportunity aplenty. Over 800,000 new businesses are started each year, most of them predicated on an idea for something new and different. Importantly, you don't have to be a genius-class inventor to cash in. Most commercially successful ideas result from *innovation*, not the rigorous, expensive, time-consuming process of *invention*.

An inventor creates something entirely new and truly unique, a "built-from-the-ground-up" item or process that never existed before. The transistor and laser are good examples. An inventor in the truest sense of the word must have an in-depth understanding of the field in which he or she is working and, given the level of sophistication our economic society has achieved, this requires substantial experience and education. Moreover, significant amounts of time and money are generally required to fuel an inventor's quest.

That's why most contemporary entrepreneurs are innovators and not inventors. Innovations are responsible for most of the commercially successful new businesses. An innovation is the combination or reconfiguration of existing items, inventions, or ideas into a new and different product, service or process. Steven Jobs and Steve Wozniak, the founders of Apple Computer, bought most of the parts for their first PC at Radio Shack. Similarly, Henry Ford was not an inventor but a master at divining consumers' needs and organizing resources and systems to meet them profitably. Horseless carriages were already on the road when Ford introduced the assembly line, standardized parts and division of labor to produce a reliable auto at an affordable price. He also pioneered the five-day workweek, an ingenious marketing innovation that eventually gave all of America's labor force another day in which they could go someplace…by auto, of course.

Ross Perot built EDS on a better way to use computer power. The McDonald brothers simply re-designed the scheme of a traditional restaurant so that it could reliably and quickly provide quality, low-cost hamburgers and milkshakes, not novel foods by any stretch of the imagination. Kemmons Wilson, the founder of Holiday Inn, just made the little "boxes" people stay in when they travel more comfortable, clean, accessible and affordable. It was a "home run" with a service that had been around since the time of Christ.

The microwave oven, ATM's, HMO's, radial tires, supermarket price scanners and cardiac defibrillators are all innovations, each the result of a clever innovator's ability to tap into existing know-how and re-assemble available technology into something new, different and valuable to consumers. Wolf Schmitt, former CEO of Rubbermaid—a company that prided itself on producing one new product a day—once observed: "The process of innovation is easy. Simply take A,B,C, and D and put them together in a new form called E."

Research shows that most successful companies are not the products of formal research or inventive genius but are simply the result of someone "discovering" an unfulfilled need in the marketplace. Therefore, your biggest challenge as an innovator is to spot a new need or find an opportunity to satisfy an existing need more efficaciously and/or economically.

Of course, you might have to do some missionary work to show that there is a need before you mobilize to profit from it. Not many people knew they "needed" a microwave oven until they were shown the magic it could perform.

As long as things continue to change, new opportunities to capitalize on those changes will emerge. Management guru Peter Drucker has said, "Innovation is the means by which entrepreneurs exploit change as an opportunity for a different business or different service. Disraeli provided the good news: "change is constant."

You can also prosper by positioning yourself to make commercial use of other inventors' ideas. The federal government spends about $75 billion annually on basic research; many large corporations spend over a billion dollars every year to devise new goods, services and processes and the technology to provide them. Much of this intellectual output is readily available to aspiring innovators.

By familiarizing yourself with the publications and Internet sites that disseminate information about newly developed inventions, technology and systems you might be able to conceive of a profitable application for the fruits of others' research prowess. This process is often referred to as "technology transfer" and most research and development organizations are interested in finding implementers with whom they can share a piece of the action. Remember, it was Bell Labs that invented the transistor, but it was SONY that used it to revolutionize the consumer electronics industry.

According to Disraeli, the secret to success in life is to "be ready for opportunity when it comes." So, hang in there, keep your eyes peeled, and stay prepared.

MUSTER YOUR CREATIVITY

Imagination rules the world.

—Napoleon, Emperor

Today, everybody places a premium on creativity.

Q. My employees, my kids, even my accountant, tell me I should be more "creative." Just what do they mean?

A. The term "creativity" is used in many ways, often inappropriately. Creativity is a subjective process whereby an innovator looks inward for thoughts, ideas and conceptual interconnections that are unique. A creative person will twist and turn chunks of information and knowledge, establishing seemingly illogical links between them.

By freely experimenting, with no heed for the traditional confines of patterns and order, you'll be able to come up with totally new constructs—ways of behaving and implementing—that can be applied to the challenges facing your enterprise. In their book, <u>Corporate Creativity</u>, professors Alan Robinson and Sam Stern assert that creativity, more than anything else, is the primary propellant of corporate growth.

The "energy" you'll need to break free and create can come only from a steady diet of new information and knowledge. These inputs must be plentiful, diverse and divergent. According to Nobel Prize winner Herbert A. Simon, creators must have abundant "relevant knowledge". Despite the fact that the average person has 50,000 thoughts per day, studies have shown that it takes about ten years of effort to acquire the 50,000 "chunks" of knowledge necessary to be reasonably creative. The more chunks, the better; the more <u>exclusive</u> the chunks, even better.

To excel in the creative process, you must know a lot about a few things and a little about a lot of things.

In-depth knowledge about a selected number of things will enable you to effectively evaluate, select and apply new good ideas to situations in which their value can be exploited. However, in order to get those new ideas in the first place, you have to be able create new syntheses that combine bits of disparate information and knowledge that have previously not been connected.

You'll have to really work to know something about a lot of things, too. Creativity consultant Steve Grossman advises erstwhile creators to read at least 50 books a year. Further, he emphasizes that at least 70% of these tomes should have nothing to do with what you do occupationally. The chief technology officer of Microsoft once "confessed" to buying about $5,000 worth of books a month through the Internet, most of which were not directly related to computer topics. By garnering a wide breadth of input, Grossman says a person is ready to create......"to make the strange familiar......to make the familiar strange."

By "toying" with both wide and narrow channels of information and knowledge, you can become a creative innovator capable of producing radically new and different discoveries and conclusions. Moreover, you'll make your kids and your accountant proud of you.

GO WITH THE RIGHT

An invasion of armies can be resisted, but not an idea whose time has come.

—Victor Hugo, Writer

Someone once said that the brain is merely an apparatus by which we *think* we think. To benefit from its extraordinary power, we must know how to use it.

Q. I've been told that, to be creative and innovative, I must learn to employ the "other side" of my brain. What does that mean?

A. To be truly creative, experts tell us that we must interrupt our habitual, super-organized, "natural" thought processes. By so doing, we can trick our brains into sidestepping their natural tendency to merely build upon what they already know. Without such deliberate interference, our brains are inclined to simply extrapolate our present awareness into "new" knowledge that, unfortunately, will not be too different from what we already have.

Edward de Bono, a renowned expert on creativity, calls this essential sidestepping process "lateral thinking." By breaking free of our normal, logical constructs for thinking, DeBono says our brain will be inclined to hook together unrelated concepts—out of sequential order—to come up with new ideas or even produce novel solutions to problems. Lateral thinking requires us to get in the way of our brain's normal functioning and force it to abandon, for the moment, its pre-ordained proclivity to pattern-making.

To accomplish such cerebral acrobatics, you have to train yourself to use both the left and right sides of your brain.

The left side of the brain provides the ability to be logical and to pursue defined opportunity step-by-step. Typically the "left brain" is verbal, analytic, symbolic, abstract, temporal, rational, digital, logical, linear, sequential, syllogistic and patterned. Research has indicated that men (notably professional managers who were trained in business schools) depend primarily on the left hemispheres of their brain. Because of its rigid, reality-focused approach, this tendency to be "concrete sequential" is not conducive to generating new ideas or different conceptual configurations.

Thinking too much with the left side will produce less-than-optimum conclusions. When making decisions, the brain unconsciously relies on the experiences and stereotypical patterns harbored in its left hemisphere, thus producing thinking that is typically conservative and extremely protective…not the stuff of which creativity is made. *(It's like getting your innovative input from your auditor!)* Rigorous, microanalysis of problems or opportunities can squeeze out right brain-based intuition, which provides us with our creative, competitive edge. From the beginning of mankind, the brain has served as a protective device, steering us clear of dangers (like the big Brontosaurus down the block) and if pushed—even in present day circumstances—it will ultimately embrace risk-avoiding conclusions.

The underused right side of the brain allows for emotionally driven pursuits. It gives us the ability to see the "whole" of a circumstance. By seeing the "big picture," we can more easily figure out how to benefit from the circumstances confronting us. Andrew S. Grove, in High Output Management, claims that creative people have an ability "to see something that is not there yet. Like an artist…looking at a blank canvas."

Here, research shows, women and entrepreneurs of both sexes excel. Positron emission tomography, a sophisticated medical imaging technique, shows that both sides of the brain flicker "on" and "off" when a person is engaged in creative thought, and it flickers most when entre-preneurs are at work. The successful entrepreneur is generally able to balance both sides in order to tap the "right side" creativity necessary to see an opportunity and the means of exploiting it while *also* being able to use the left side to devise the methods necessary to organize and direct the resources required for implementation.

The "right brain" is nonverbal, synthetic, free, analogic, non-tempo-ral, non-rational, spatial, intuitive, holistic, serendipitous, and unen-cumbered. Get the picture??

Brass Tacks Tip: A successful entrepreneurial leader must be able to rapidly and frequently switch back and forth between hemispheres of the brain, integrating the products of each. Obviously, everyone does some switching in order to function in everyday life, but generally one side—typically the left side—is dominant. To be maximally innova-tive, you must come as close as biologically possible to over-riding left side dominance.

Legend has it that Einstein, when he and his team were stumped at the beginning of the day as to which intellectual direction to follow during that day's activity, always *forced* the right side of his brain into action to choose the most aesthetic option.

Keep in mind that creativity—or *"thinking out of the box"*—often requires deliberate action to overcome what we have learned. Most of our formal education concentrates on improving the performance of the left side of our brain. Indeed, studies show that a child's creativity drops almost 90% between the ages of five and seven, the period in which formal education first intrudes. The process continues as we age and "learn." By the age of forty, the typical person has only 2% of the creativity he or she possessed just prior to entering school.

The atmosphere of the "normal" corporate world also tends to retard creativity. Creativity guru Gordon MacKenzie, a thirty-year vet-eran of Hallmark, once equated corporate bureaucracy to a giant hair-ball that doesn't allow much space for thinking and creativity. The institutional tendency to rely on the past as the primary guide to the future, he said, creates a Gordian Knot of normalcy that grows in mass and gravitational pull over time. The creative innovator, therefore, must constantly use both sides of his or her brain to break free from the entangling and retarding nature of "the hairball."

FOLLOW THE SHIFT

I skate to where the puck will be, not where it is.
> —Wayne Gretzky, Hockey player

Many business leaders revere "market share" as some sort of Holy Grail. Fact is, there's another measure of company performance that's much more relevant in today's rapidly changing world.

Q. I've been told that my company's market share is the most important indicator of its present and future success. Just what percentage of the market do I have to control in order to keep ahead of the pack?

A. A goal of 100% would be nice, but hardly ever achievable and never practical. However, something short of complete control of the market is a worthy goal, since studies have shown that profitability is directly related to market share. The bigger piece of the market action you control, the more you can influence pricing, promotion, customer awareness, the costs of what you buy and the channels of distribution that are important in your markets. Share of market also constitutes a meaningful, visible goal for management and sales personnel. Many firms gear their compensation programs to performance with respect to market share. A healthy market share, therefore, is something to be desired.

Market share can be measured in several ways. The difficult part is finding out what the total market is. This can be done by determining total dollar sales (the most common indicator) or stats like units sold, customers served, or transactions processed in the entire market targeted by you and your direct competitors. The gauge you choose to measure market share depends on the nature of your industry and the dimensions that are most relevant to your operation and your bottom line.

Once you know the aggregate pot that everyone is fighting over, you can simply relate your firm's specific accomplishments to the total. The resulting percentage is your share.

For many companies, market share has assumed an unhealthy prominence. While I buy into its importance as a performance indicator—one among many—I'm less sanguine about its ability to accurately reflect a firm's posture and prospects with respect to the <u>emerging</u> market. Market share statistics constitute a snapshot, a picture of the firm's position *at a given point in time*. While the smart decisions and momentum that got the firm to that spot might—I emphasize *might*—keep it moving on a trajectory that allows it to remain in the forefront of the market as presently defined, it says nothing about how the firm will fare as the market metamorphoses.

While a healthy piece of the market that existed yesterday can provide a sound launching pad for future activity, it by no means will guarantee continued good performance in the new markets that are emerging. Markets are constantly shifting and it is incumbent upon a firm to secure a respectable piece of that shift as well. As a consequence, I tend to give as much weight—in most cases, more—to a firm's ability to attain "share of market shift" as I do to its achievements with respect to static "market share."

Things are happening so quickly in today's dynamic global economy that the market that existed yesterday can be abandoned in a blink of an eye by an innovative vendor that makes significant changes in the way that the old market's value was produced and delivered to customers. As a consequence, a firm that did well in the old market may not even be a player in the new market.

Ironically, a firm's share of the old market might actually increase as a more innovative competitor pulls out and creates a new market within which it will seek a dominant position. So while the slower contender's share of the old market might rise from 40 to 60% overnight, the relevance and potential of that particular market *overall* could very well be greatly diminished by the emergence of the new playing field. The new market that emerges might be much more important, profitable and promising than the old turf.

A good example can be found in the case of Microsoft. While Bill Gates was building his share of the PC operating system market, a couple of other upstarts came along and shifted the real action into the arena of the Internet. Bill had to work long and hard to get a respectable share of that shifted market.

Brass Tacks Tip: Exclusive focus on existing market share will incline a company to fight over the bones of an aging carcass, while its more innovative competitors will have already begun a new hunt for "fresh meat." Sole focus on share of market in the "here and now" dimension will cause a firm to limit its struggle to pricing, promotion, delivery and service for the things that *already exist.* To be truly successful in this age, a company must focus on the *next* "order of things," the fundamentally *new* products or services that they must offer to remain competitive. As a consequence, successful owners and managers must strive for the all-important "share of market shift" that will determine the winners and losers in an ever-evolving marketplace.

STRIVE TO BREAKOUT

Some men see things as they are and say "why?" I dream things that never were and say "why not?"

—Robert Kennedy, Senator

Corporations, like people, follow a natural cycle of birth, growth, maturity and expiration. But, artificial enterprises, like business firms, have a unique advantage. Living creatures with souls and socks, like you and me, have pretty limited opportunities to extend our actuarially estimated life expectancies. However, corporations can—with innovative management and luck—stretch their years of life for decades beyond normal expectations.

Q. I am the CEO and largest shareholder of a large, publicly-traded corporation that is well respected as a "growth" company that supposedly has a lot of "promise." Unfortunately, I see warts that others don't. We haven't come up with a truly different product in years. I've tried to extend our company's life cycle by deliberately trying to destroy the old ways of doing things but, no matter how hard I try, we can't seem to get on an innovative roll. Any ideas???

A. Innovation is easier said than done. Indeed, there are some very good reasons why most companies—even the high-tech darlings of just a few years ago—can't seem to muster the innovative behavior necessary to perpetuate their good fortune.

Essentially, an innovation is a significant change in the way an enterprise mobilizes its resources to create value. There are two basic planes of innovation.

One is "performance innovation" which involves efforts to improve or make better in some way the fundamental, already established products or processes that are the hallmarks of the innovating firm. Adding new features, improving quality, re-figuring pricing, reducing delivery time, or enhancing support service are among some of the innovative changes a company can implement to upgrade performance. Generally, these kinds of alterations won't shift a company from a slow growth pattern to a faster pace of expansion. At best, they tend to extend a firm's period of maturation, letting it hang in there a bit longer before hitting the slippery slide to eventual extinction. Interestingly, most large, successful companies seem to focus almost all of their energies on performance innovation.

The other type of innovation—the kind that truly makes a difference in the fortunes of a firm—is "breakout innovation." This involves development efforts that go beyond "new" into the realm of "different"—*very different*. Indeed, this kind of self-reinvention is essential if a firm wishes to avoid the vulnerabilities associated with maturity, the second last stage of natural evolution. Economist Joseph Schumpeter called it "creative destruction," i.e. the dissembling and discarding of the old, established—albeit currently successful—ways of doing things before there is perceptible pressure to do so. Schumpeter advocated fixing things before they are broken, at exactly the point in a firm's growth and expansion trajectory where everyone is comfortable and sublimely happy about how things are going.

A firm can launch a new era of substantive vitality for itself by commencing a fresh cycle of activity that involves a significantly different product, service, process or way of doing things. The good news is that it can embark on this promising journey without giving up what it is currently doing, so long as the capital it is employing is being put to its highest and best use.

Needless to say, this kind of innovation is difficult to pull off. No one likes to tinker with a well-running machine, especially if there is no guarantee that the tinkering will pay off in the short run. But, breakout innovation is absolutely essential if a firm desires to perpetuate its growth and postpone the treacherous infirmity associated with maturity. Indeed, the inability to make this innovative leap is the primary reason that most firms get terminally "long in the tooth" and eventually disappear.

Such a transition in the affairs of a firm requires the vision, courage, risk-taking tolerance and seat-of-the-pants verve of a dyed-in-the-wool entrepreneur. A traditionally trained manager—even one boasting a gilt-edged MBA—won't make it happen unless he or she harbors—and uses—the fire-in-the-belly spirit of a true entrepreneur.

This process of re-invention in the face of current, acceptable company performance creates what Clayton Christensen calls the "innovator's dilemma." In his book of the same name, he alleges that "many of what are now widely accepted principles of good management are, in fact, only situationally appropriate." He claims there are times at which it is not right to pursue a path of normalcy, to listen attentively to customers, to follow a "rational" plan. Conversely, he says, there are times when "it is right to invest in developing lower performance products that promise lower margins, and right to aggressively pursue small, rather than substantial, markets."

Pity the poor contemporary manager. All of the things he's learned about planning and execution, all of the things his customers are presently demanding, all of the strategies that inventors and bankers want to see, and all of the "fine-tuning" his employees are endeavoring to implement might very well lead him into a pattern of performance that sets his firm up as a vulnerable target for a new, more entrepreneurially energized start-up.

Performance innovation is essential, but it isn't enough. While it will help make a firm better at what it is doing, the real key to competitive survival in this day and age involves doing some things very, very differently.

Today's manager must determine just what mix of evolutionary performance innovation and revolutionary breakout innovation is required to fuel its future progress and prosperity.

LOOK BEYOND CUSTOMER'S DEMANDS

Originality is the only thing that counts.

—George Gershwin, Composer

Continuous, baby step improvements in a company's performance—generally referred to as "performance innovation"—simply don't give a firm the power, position and presence it needs to prevail in the face of torrid competition form entrepreneurially-driven start-ups who are offering significantly different, superior value.

Q. I've just finished a book that advocates dramatic "breakout innovation" over the much more predictable and manageable "performance innovation." I've long believed that more rational, incremental and extrapolative change is more readily welcomed by customers than cosmic efforts to generate goods or services that are *very, very* different than what is currently offered. Am I off base?

A. Yes. Such change might be more readily welcomed, but it generally isn't in your best long-term interests. Slow change that's tightly conditioned by historical patterns is unable to produce the kinds of truly different utilities that customers *will* want in the near term future. Furthermore, companies that rely solely on performance innovation eventually become incapable of accommodating the dramatic shifts in market demand that occur with ever-increasing frequency in today's e-world. For example, traditional department stores have done a fine job expanding selection, convenience, price options and personal customer care. But, they have failed to embrace the true breakout innovations in logistics management, auction-pricing, category aggregating and Internet marketing that have made WalMart, eBay, and Best Buy the threatening competitive powerhouses that they are today.

This isn't new news. Henry Ford didn't just build a better automobile; he created an entirely new way of manufacturing, marketing and financing personal transportation for an entirely different segment of the population. Breakout innovation!

On the other hand, performance innovation, the incremental process of simply improving—very gradually—what already exists, tends to follow the trajectories of yesterday. While such changes enhance what is, they don't create what *should be* to meet the needs of tomorrow.

This tendency toward gradual—often glacial—change is compounded by the ingrained habit of "well-trained" managers to analyze *current* trends to divine *the future*. Unfortunately, trends are rooted in the past; they're extrapolations of what used to be. These proximate paths are attractive to managers nevertheless because they can be seen much more clearly than expectations that depend on a "crystal ball" and right-brain calisthenics.

Trend analysis can provide *some* helpful stimulation and input, but a manager concerned with the future must deliberately insulate himself against the channeled visioning that is a natural byproduct of over-reliance on trend tracking.

Breakout innovation requires truly unfettered speculation about what *could be;* what is *possible*, not probable. Here, fantasization is more important than fact gathering; a crystal ball more productive than focus groups. Creative thinking, a la the prescriptions of Alex Osborne, must be the order of the day for a leader who wants the "first mover" advantages that come with breaking into new, fertile territories that aren't cluttered with competitors.

Alas, when it comes to strategizing, "well-trained" managers too often revert to the lessons learned in B-school and bring to bear the big guns of market research. Generally, this consists of listening intently to the expressed needs of *existing* customers. (After all, most managers have been trained to conceptually put these customers at the top of their organization charts.)

While this type of customer positioning certainly is appropriate when it comes to selling today's product today, or providing superior customer service, it doesn't hack it when it comes to envisioning the future.

Prevailing customer attitudes generally don't favor breakout innovation. That's because customers typically see the world in their rear-view mirrors. They know what they've grown to like and what they want (for now, at least). They are familiar with the way it is delivered and they have a routine for dealing with the prevailing vendor/customer inter-connection. As a consequence, in the face of a "survey" they often provide reassuring feedback that deludes a vendor's market research team into thinking that a customer's expressions of satisfaction are indicative of enduring, immutable convictions. Researchers reasonably conclude that, "since the customer is comfortable with what we are presently doing, it would be foolish to try and significantly change something in our delivered utility,—even if *we* feel it would constitute a move in a better direction." The "customer is king" syndrome generally signals that it would be folly to fix what isn't broke.

Even big business customers don't encourage breakthrough innovations among their suppliers, since they have an enormous investment in doing things the way they were done yesterday. At any given point in time, a customer's processes, systems, and product configurations are established to mesh with the utilities a vendor is providing *at that point in time.* It is believed that changes instigated by a vendor will translate into necessary—perhaps inconvenient, untimely and even expensive—requisite changes on the part of the customer. Consequently customers are quick to let a vendor know that any change should be on their terms, in their time frame.

Problem is, these consumers will change their tune in a heartbeat when a new entrepreneur comes to market with a cheaper, better and truly different thingamajig that delivers better value at lower cost—something that forces them to change in the face of murderous competitive pressure.

So, *"seller beware!"* When a customer eventually hears the message of a new, hard-charging entrant in the marketplace and decides that's the way to go, it's usually too late for the established vendor of record to make the changes necessary to keep the relationship.

Don't delude yourself into thinking that won't happen. In the words of Georges Deroit, father of modern venture capital financing: "There will always be someone, somewhere, doing something designed to put you out of business."

Brass Tacks Tip: Don't assume that the customer is always right; never underestimate the role of the "fickle factor" in customer relationships.

Indeed, by relying on performance innovations, an established vendor of record can actually push his customers to the "breakout innovation" of a new competitor. This is how PC makers pulled the rug out from under IBM mainframes in the 1980's. Many once dominant firms like Wang, Woolworth, and WordPerfect simply did not survive intact in the face of the dramatic "siren songs" of breakout innovation.

FIND THE PATHS

It is a bad plan that admits of no modification.

—Popular maxim, circa 100 AD

Q. Our company creates a new long-term plan every five years or so. Problem is, by the end of the first six months, a lot of things have changed; and by the end of the first year, the plan is virtually useless. So, why plan?

A. Good point. Comprehensive long-term plans—the experts call them "strategic" plans—that aren't flexible, fluid, "living" guides become rapidly obsolete and frequently counterproductive. Too many of us, in our desire for security and predictability, tend to see plans as *prescriptions* for action, dictates that must be followed come hell or high water. Today, with a rapidly accelerating pace of change in all quarters, we can't allow ourselves to be trapped into the lock-step regimen of a rigid plan.

Indeed, in today's business world, a good alternative to old-fashioned planning is *Pathfinding,*™ a fluid, serendipitous, exploitative process by which an organization can move forward year-by-year, accomplishment-by-accomplishment, taking advantage of unforeseen opportunity and mastering unpredictable challenges as it moves ahead.

To be sure, it's best to start a journey with a map, a deliberately designed itinerary that looks good at the point of embarkation and has a reasonable probability of getting you to where you want to go. But once you set sail, your speed and direction is going to be determined by the prevailing wind. A lot of unplanned trimming and tacking may be necessary. As you move along, you might even find the opportunity to head for a different, more rewarding destination.

This is not to say that planning, in the traditional sense, is not important. All organizations and every individual within them should have a vision of the future they desire and some carefully formulated intentions with respect to attaining it. These aims are typically laid out as prescribed goals and tactics in the organization's annual business plan, a classic "set piece" for action. In this sense, plans provide a necessary framework to guide activity.

But it must be a malleable framework. Planners cannot be blind to the serendipity of real life. My ol' uncle Ollie used to say: "Planning is something that keeps you busy while life is happening to you."

It's important, therefore, to employ plan formats that invite updating and revision as time passes and experience is gathered. Planning is a continuing process, not a once-a-year exercise.

I am inclined to equate it more with pathfinding than with prescribing. A pathfinder will follow the map as long as it makes sense and travel conditions are favorable. But he or she will also be sensitive to shortcuts and new opportunities for a more rewarding course. The ability to capitalize on situations as they emerge and to exploit good fortune when it occurs gives a pathfinder's firm a tremendous competitive edge.

As any good infantry leader will attest, "plans are great until the first shot is fired." Once in the fray, victory, to a great degree, is discovered by accident. Importantly, these kinds of discoveries can only be successfully exploited by opportunists who are well prepared, have a keen eye and are ever ready to take advantage of emerging circumstances.

Often referred to as 'luck," these actions are actually a result of "preparedness colliding with opportunity." Such fortuitous "matchings" are not predictable enough to be mandated or precisely scheduled within a plan. At the time a plan is developed, these events may only be "possible" or, at best, "probable." Maybe, they're just a dream. Indeed, many opportunities aren't even conceived of prior to their happening.

It is important, nonetheless, for a corporate pathfinder to speculate about these "potentialities" and prepare to shift resources to take advantage of them if and when they materialize. Trend scanning, brainstorming, the construction of "what if" scenarios, and the use of Delphi exercises can help planners anticipate opportunities that they should be ready to exploit. As Thomas Edison insisted: "Chance favors the prepared mind." Today, we call it "catching a wave." Careful analysis, speculation, and a deliberate use of intuition can help an organization's leaders seize unique opportunities and gain distinct advantages vis-à-vis a competitor.

A strategic planner must map out both prescribed paths and possible paths in order to take advantage of circumstances that are predictable or contingent. Here, success depends on an organization's distinctive "competencies." To effectively choose optimum paths of action, an organization's leaders must have a firm appreciation of its unique abilities and capacities. These special, proprietary strengths must be thoroughly understood so that they can be effectively paired with opportunities that emerge along the path from *present circumstances* to *desired future.*

PROMPT YOURSELF

Discovery consists of seeing what everybody has seen and thinking what nobody has thought.

—Albert von Szent-Gyorgyi, Biochemist

To a creative artist, there is nothing more challenging than a huge, blank canvas.

Q. I am about to prepare the first business plan for my growing company. Is there any kind of a planning checklist available that would ensure that I am covering all of the bases with respect to issues and opportunities I should consider??

A. Not too long ago, the Center for Business Ownership Inc. developed a *Self√Check*™ offering a wide range of action "prompts" that will help a planner focus on the key strategies and tactics that should be included in any business plan.

Each of these *"c/prompts"* is a word that will suggest—to an open, curious and creative mind—an *activity* that can influence, in some way, to some degree, a firm's attainment of relevant, worthy goals.

By juxtaposing each of these *"c/prompts"* to every major line item in your firm's preliminary cash flow projections, a variety of ideas will come to mind with respect to possible operational goals, projects, practices, procedures and techniques that can be included in your final plan. This word association exercise will encourage consideration of a wide range of issues with respect to each critical cash-generating or cash-using function of your company. Since cash is the pervasive lifeblood of any enterprise, the *c/prompts* will force you to directly relate intended actions to those factors that are most important to the success of your firm.

Let's say you decide to relate the "critical advantage" prompt to every line of your cash flow or profit-and-loss statement. As a consequence, you would be induced to consider the impact of your firm's distinctive characteristics (its penchant for outstanding quality, for example) to such controllable performance determinants as sales, returns, labor costs, equipment requirements and the like. Accordingly, the plans you formulate would take into consideration these critical items. Another example might involve the special human talent your firm requires and the impact that that important element has on wages, benefits and special compensation plans, like employee stock options.

As you progress down the list of *c/prompts* and match them to individual cash flow line items, you will be prompted to contemplate an expanding array of opportunities for action that can be included in your plan.

The *c/prompt* mechanism will help clarify the "web" of interconnections between your strategic goals and the cash-impacting tactical maneuvers your firm might consider. After a bit of financial triage, those activities that you conclude would have the most positive top and bottom line impact on your firm would be top candidates for inclusion in your plan.

Offered below is a list of *c/prompts* that will stimulate such line-by-line consideration.

CUSTOMERS: Since "nothing happens 'til somebody sells something," the genesis of any enterprise must be the revenue stream it derives from sales. The "top line" is the "magic" that only entrepreneurial leaders can produce. Consequently, any business plan must begin with a vision of the exact composition of the headwater of the revenue stream, i.e. its customers and their desires.

CAPACITY: To produce the utilities that are "needed" by a market, a firm must mobilize and fully employ the resources available to it. Its plan must provide for the optimal application of the entire range of its resources—from hard assets like plants and machinery to intangibles like knowledge, organizational structure and the pattern of leadership.

CONTRIBUTORS: Many constituencies impact the value-creating activities of a business enterprise. These individual and institutional providers must be carefully identified, recruited, employed and stimulated. A well-crafted business plan will provide for the application of appropriate talents to prevailing opportunities.

CONDITIONERS: Your ambitious plans will be shaped greatly by internal and external conditions, conventions and cultural influences. Only rarely can these factors be clearly defined, but since each of these items can impact a firm significantly, they must be adequately considered in the planning process.

CONTROLS: The controls that a firm adopts will have a determinative effect on the course of its development. As a result, all of the probable needs for systems and methods of control must be taken into account, and your plan must provide for their development and use.

CRITICAL ADVANTAGE: To survive and thrive in today's marketplace, *and do it better than the competition,* a firm must enjoy one or more critical advantages. These "edges" enable a firm to be a unique contender. Every special capacity of your firm (i.e. its "distinctive competencies") should be related to specific, desired financial outcomes in your plan.

CONSTRAINTS: Every organism has limits, either self-imposed or levied by external forces. These boundaries should be thoroughly considered as you prepare your plans. In some cases, these constraints can be favorably changed or influenced; in other situations, they will be fast and firm. Whatever their nature, they must be dealt with in the planning process and their impacts figured into the proposed strategies and tactics of your firm.

COMPARISONS: In order to plot a truly competitive course, a firm must divine its position relative to all of its competitors, both existing and emerging. This can be accomplished by getting a "fix" on all influential externals and formulating an estimate of how their expected actions will impact your intentions as expressed in your plan.

CONTINGENCIES: In all endeavors—even those that are well conceived and meticulously planned—things tend to "go bump in the night." Unforeseen or unanticipated events can push a venture dramatically off course. While adroit management *might* be able to compensate for such happenings, the most effective defense against the negative effects of such shocks consists of well-planned, contingency countermeasures. Make sure you have a backup strategy with respect to each key assumption in your cash flow plans.

If the above factors are weighed carefully in the light of each expected inflow and outflow of cash, you will generate more than enough worthy strategies and tactics for your plan.

PLAN TO PLAN

There is no royal road to anything. One thing at a time, and all things in succession.

—William Jennings Bryan, Politician and orator

"Worthwhile results depend on worthwhile plans" is a truism that has guided American business enterprises for generations. It's still valid today, but the type of plan required has changed considerably.

Q. Every couple of years I try to hammer out a new plan for my business. A while back you wrote that "Pathfinding" was better than planning. How so?

A. Plans are still essential to performance, but a new type of planning process is required in this era of rapid change and fierce competition. In the old days, the boss could stipulate a bunch of objectives, rally the troops, give everybody their marching orders, and, if the goals were worthy, sit back to monitor rather predictable progress. Nowadays, a business plan must combine both tactical *and* strategic elements and be *cooperatively* crafted to accommodate several time dimensions.

Today's plans must be more inclusive, ambitious and fluid. Further, they must be formulated by the people expected to implement them. Plans also must be amenable to creative change as problems and opportunities emerge. In other words, planning must be an on-going *participative* process that is *exploitative* in nature.

Indeed, the word "planning" suggests precision and predictability, generally unachievable attributes in this day and age. Old-fashioned planning closely resembles the kind of thing generals do before a battle.

Contemporary planning is more closely akin to the type of quick, responsive, ingenious thinking that propels a platoon leader to victory once the battle has started.

I call this type of preparation and implementation *Pathfinding.* ™ A pathfinder has objectives and intentions, but is always open to on-the-spot modifications—bred of good fortune or bad luck—that will allow him to find better means to the ends sought…or even better ends if the possibility presents itself.

The old planning paradigm consisted of 1) goals (usually handed down from above); 2) narrowly-defined activities designed to achieve those ends; and 3) a time frame in which this was all to be accomplished. Once one plan had expired—usually after twelve months of muddled aspiration and frustration—a new one was created.

I know of many companies that boast linear feet of shelf space devoted to the annual plans of yesteryear. These books are testaments to "push planning," i.e. the struggle through which resources are pointed in the direction of a desired objective and "pushed" relentlessly until they reach it or until the plan is "modified." In this kind of planning endeavor, digression from the plotted itinerary is despised and vast amounts of time, expense and energy are expended "staying the course," pushing the great rock of Sisyphus in the direction of the sought-after pinnacle.

In this era of irrepressible change, plans must be continuously "in process." Simultaneous formulation and implementation are essential, and the entire process must be punctuated from time to time by team efforts to re-formulate or re-define the ultimate objectives. In this paradigm, pathfinders are *pulled* to their objectives, mastering the unexpected events that are serendipitously encountered along the way. Change is embraced and exploited.

This new, dynamic approach to forging the future is different from traditional planning in many ways.

• It requires the enlightened participation of _all_ of an organization's constituents. They must be involved in both the formulation of goals and the design of intended interim activities that will lead to the achievement of their selected ends. Each participant has to be well informed and must have access to other participants, the firm's customers, and all relevant financial information pertaining to the enterprise.

- It requires no less than two or more than five central goals that are inclusive, visionary, ambitious and unfettered.

- It must be based on, and take full advantage of, the _unique competencies_ of the enterprise as discovered and defined by its constituents.

- It has to allow for on-the-spot exploitation of opportunity and confrontation of threats. The leaders and followers of the enterprise must feel empowered to criticize current activity and suggest new approaches. This requires on-going, open communication and knowledge sharing. Everyone must feel free to act immediately and decisively when situations warrant, without the fear of retribution or second-guessing.

- Its thrust of accomplishment must take into account that every group activity has both "fences" and "gates" which provide broad parameters for action _and_ the freedom to go beyond when advantageous.

- It demands an organizational culture that will tolerate one or more—often completely different—organizational structures, depending on the mission and the resources deployed. Whatever the constellation, however, it requires any group of involved implementers to function as a team.

- It requires _entrepreneurial leaders_ who are innovative and can emulate the drive, creativity, industriousness and sense of mission that marked the original founders of the enterprise. Leaders and followers must personally identify with the fundamental purposes of the entity, not just its specific, delimited "goals du jour."

- It begs a tolerance for uncertainty, ambiguousness, eccentricity, risk-taking and failure.

- It must promote—and accommodate—ultra-swift action.

- It needs intuitive operatives who can recognize and take advantage of luck.

- It must allow for—but not be driven by—specific protocols that guide short-term implementation.

- It must be both formulated and executed by individuals who have a true sense of personal _ownership_ in the enterprise. Actual and "virtual" ownership techniques can be used to provide the motivation and approbation that is required.

Pathfinding™ promotes the kind of "creative destruction" and "constructive innovation" that modern enterprises need to stay relevant and competitive.

Brass Tacks Tip: Worthwhile results depend on participating, pumped-up, purpose-driven Pathfinders!

EXPECT RESISTANCE

Everyone thinks of changing the world, but no one thinks of changing himself.

—Leo Tolstoy, Political Leader

"Change is the law," observed President John F. Kennedy. But, as hard as we might try to observe a new law or accommodate a new change, it's often difficult to overcome the negative feelings created by these "bumps" in our established way of life.

Q. I own a business that is constantly changing in big ways and at a fast pace. I take time to logically explain the reasons for these events to my employees, but they seem to be getting more and more resistant as time passes. I can't stop change; how can I convince them to get with the program?

A. Too often we get caught up with the facts of the change and overlook the powerful feelings that new and different ways of doing things can engender. Resistance to change—even positive change that will be good for everybody—is common, and a good manager has to be ready to cope with it constructively. Bertrand Russell observed: "Change is one thing; progress is another." As a boss you are responsible for converting change to progress, but it won't happen unless you can get your team members to accept, adopt and productively exploit the changes you are promoting.

Indeed, in the early stages of a significant change, you should be proactively looking for signs of resistance. It's easy to misinterpret employees' early shock and numbness as ready compliance. Also, many employees are inclined to believe "if we ignore it, it'll go away." As a result, what looks like—to a perpetrator of change—"slam dunk" acceptance is really a false veneer that belies the personal turmoil and sense of loss that exists. You cannot simply "get on with business as usual" after you introduce disruptive change. If you don't persist in your efforts to achieve genuine understanding and acceptance, wary feelings among your constituents will turn to rock solid resistance.

Accordingly, any significant change requires you to provide caring, continuing assistance with the transition—even if it looks like everybody has bought into the plan.

Employees need time to sort out their fears and doubts, to talk over the probable impacts, and to say good-bye to the past. And all the while, they need you to reaffirm the wisdom and inevitability of the change, to show empathy (while not in any way bad-mouthing the change) and to demonstrate a willingness to do all you can to make the adoption process palatable and personally productive.

Remember, change can be extremely threatening and can create serious self-doubt, depression, anxiety and frustration. At the very least, those affected by change will feel a loss of security, as the competence they achieved in dealing with the old ways will no longer be relevant. Their "territory" will have been invaded, and their relationships upset. Their sense of direction will be lost and, worst case, their sense of identity diminished. For many, this sense of loss can approximate the trauma associated with the death of a friend. These are real feelings and can't be easily overcome. (With feelings like this abounding, you can imagine what is happening to productivity!) That's why it's helpful to get people to talk and express their feelings and fears. Both group meetings and one-on-one discussions are appropriate.

It will take time, but eventually the affected workers will begin to carefully examine the dimensions of the new reality in their lives. They'll try to figure out exactly what it means and how it will touch them. They'll begin to test the new circumstance. The will try to figure out how they'll fit, how they will relate to others, and, very importantly, how they might actually *benefit* from the change. Here again, it is important for you to be attentive and supportive. Organizing your charges into teams will aid in establishing individual and organizational commitment to "the new way." Keep them focused on the short-term goals and priorities that they can easily relate to. Be generous with praise and rewards for those who become early, enthusiastic converts. Encourage experimentation on the premise "try it, you'll like it."

Finally, your employees will see some clear, achievable goals, and they'll begin to appreciate that these outcomes will be beneficial to them as well as the company. It is critical that you help them gain some feeling of control with respect to the new future that is emerging. Here's where formal planning sessions—with *everyone* participating—can produce big results. If your team members can feel that they are the architects of the future, they will be more inclined to believe that they'll be safe and comfortable living in that future.

Brass Tacks Tip: Since change will be the only constant in our future, your efforts to aid workers in coping with change must be ongoing. Your job description should specifically include a perpetual responsibility to be a "handmaiden to change."

Importantly, a pre-established, well-demonstrated atmosphere of trust will go a long way toward helping your team members to confidently and productively reach out and embrace the future as it is unfolding.

USE YOUR GUT

The best of seers is he who guesses well.

—Euripides, Dramatist

College professors tell us that the best decisions are products of analysis, reflection and careful consideration. Problem is, this approach requires time, a commodity that's always in short supply. Moreover, such traditional scientific decision-making tends to stifle creativity, the avenue to innovative action that can produce salutary effects beyond those related to the decision at hand.

Q. Seems like the pace of everything in the business world is increasing daily. In the old days, I had time to ponder my moves before committing myself to a course of action. Today, as you wrote, it's "ready, fire, aim." I'm depending more and more on my gut feeling. Is this a trend or is this just me??

A. You're not alone. Intuition is no longer the exclusive purview of females and oracles. The press of time and the importance of innovation have prompted entrepreneurs and managers to ever more frequently "go with their guts" when it's time to fish or cut bait.

Over two hundred years ago, the Fourth Earl of Chesterfield, an English statesman and man of letters, exclaimed: "We, my lords, may thank Heaven that we have something better than our brains to depend on." He was referring to intuition, that ethereal, gut-based ability possessed by everyone but used by few.

A response to intuitive urges is not to be confused with "finger to the wind" guessing. Intuition is a much more powerful tool than mere guessing. Each of us is, in fact, blessed with an "inner voice" that, if properly developed and responded to, can be a big assist when we're faced with making a decision without all of the facts and analyses we'd like to have. Intuition is a valuable personal faculty that can produce powerful positive results in any business environment.

Definitions of intuition abound: " Knowledge gained without rational thought; Feeling based on past experiences buried in the subconscious; Knowing by direct insight or cognition without the use of inference; The act or faculty of knowing directly; Sparks of spontaneous thought that are produced without the benefit of facts or logic."

Essentially, intuition is a capacity to formulate effective insights, expectations or courses of action *without* having all of the facts and *without* having performed a complete analysis of the prevailing situation. It's accumulated knowledge that's buried in our subconscious. Occasionally, it bubbles up to our consciousness where it can be put to work. It is important stuff but, unfortunately, it's stuck back in the recesses of our psyche along with our dreams. Consequently, it can't be called up at will like deliberately filed and indexed memories.

However we define them, these "vibes" not only help us make decisions more quickly but also enable us to conceive answers and actions that are more creative, unique, inspired and powerful than we could ever evoke through routine analysis. Psychologist Carl Jung calls intuition one of the four basic psychological functions, along with thinking, feeling and sensation.

The payoffs can be enormous. Ted Turner attributes the creation of his revolutionary 24-hour news format to gut feeling. Similar acknowledgments have been made by Steve Jobs, creator of the Apple Computer, John Reed, former CEO of Citicorp, and Fred Smith, founder of Federal Express. The engineers at Chrysler credited their intuition with decisions that helped them develop and introduce the successful minivan concept before General Motors and Ford. Appreciating the importance of intuition, companies like General Foods, Shell Oil, Phillips Petroleum, Proctor & Gamble and Digital Equipment Corp.

have supported the development of intuitive skills among their managers.

Tests conducted by Professor Weston H. Igor, a pioneer in the study of intuition, demonstrated that, without exception, the top managers in every organization rated significantly higher than middle or lower-level managers in their ability to use intuition on the job. The important point here is that this power is not conferred to CEOs as a rite of passage; it is a potency that, if frequently accessed by ambitious people, actually helps propel them to the top of their enterprises.

The power of intuition comes from deep within us. Experts tell us that much of what we know, we do not know we know. It's stored away in the remote recesses of our subconscious. Acquired, initially, as the instincts of our ancestors were passed on to us genetically, it is supplemented later in life by experiences we have but don't deliberately log into our readily accessible memories. This is rare knowledge that, if mustered and applied in contemporary circumstances, can facilitate faster, better, more distinctive decisions and enable us to conceptualize and create in superior ways.

Unfortunately, we cannot command this resource to our use at will. It typically "bubbles to the surface" spontaneously when certain circumstances or stimuli are present. The trick, therefore, is to create an inviting atmosphere that will attract this powerful "visitor" to our psyche.

The biggest obstacle to our productive use of intuition is our own skepticism. Most of us believe it is impossible to "know" without going through all of the hoops of learning, evaluating and analyzing. All of our lives we are encouraged to favor deductive reasoning over inductive reasoning and, to this day, many companies still reinforce this regressive preference by allocating their employee performance rewards accordingly.

From childhood, we are taught that "responsible" people depend upon knowledge, reason and analysis to make their decisions. It's easy to buy into this "logic." After all, who wants to attribute the good results of a decision to luck? What manager wants to tell the boss that a bad decision was due to gut feeling? It's much safer to minimize our personal responsibility by applying old-fashioned, tried-and-true rules, routines and reactionary reason. This is safe but not smart because, as a consequence, the "eureka" benefits of *instinctive* action are lost.

Here are some **Brass Tacks Tip: s** for facilitating circumstances in which intuitive power can be called forth and productively applied.

- Believe in it: Our beliefs about our capabilities determine what we, indeed, can do. It is important, therefore to learn as much as we can about intuition and how it can be exploited. Among the better books on this topic are Awakening Intuition by Frances E. Vaughn (Anchor Press/Doubleday) and Practical Intuition by Laura Day (Villard Books/Random House). It's sometimes difficult to counter Sgt. Friday's universally accepted dictum—"Just the facts, Ma'am"—but, to seize the competitive advantage, we must learn to supplement the traditional analytical tools that can take us just so far. To accomplish this, we have to identify the beliefs we have that block intuitive activity and get rid of them. Sometimes your intuition might even go against what your own reason tells you is right. In these cases, a trust in your intuitive self, bred of good experience, is particularly important.

- Track your success: Take note of when your hunches pay off; compile a record of evidence over the long term. Post-hunch verification and testing is important. Make an effort to remember those times when you "just knew" something that later turned out to be true. Good experiences will reinforce your propensity to trust your gut. Over time, they will also suggest the kinds of circumstances that are most conducive to the effective use of your intuition.

- Experiment: Grab every opportunity to test your hunches, even in situations where the outcome is not central to what you are doing. These "freebies" are chances to gauge your intuition without risking a serious negative consequence. Observe day-to-day events and activities of others, mentally speculating about what will happen. Then score your hunches. These harmless exercises will give you feedback about what works for you and what doesn't.

• <u>Learn the signals</u>: Be sensitive to the clues your body gives to its readiness to make a successful intuitive leap. People have reported all kinds of signs, e.g. hair standing up on the back of the neck, goose bumps, sweaty palms, a churning tummy, a tiny "voice," rapid eye blinking, even visions that are flashed on the inside of the forehead. Zero in on these bridges between your conscious and subconscious. They can increase your batting average considerably.

• <u>Drop the barriers</u>: It has been shown that while a person can remember about 50,000 words, phrases or chess moves, he can't remember more then seven *unrelated* things at a time. So if you want your intuition to ascend into your right brain consciousness, you have to give it room. Clear out the clutter of currently pressing issues. Look beyond the immediate crisis. Relax, get comfortable, and create a "blank screen" on which your "third hand" can write. Practice maintaining an open-minded, experimental, non-judgmental attitude. Daydreaming is good. Wait for the missing piece of the puzzle to pop up. Drop any barriers to your receptivity to such impulses or spontaneous stimuli. While it is impossible to maintain this posture exclusively for 24-hours a day, set aside times when you try *not* to think; just pay attention to what "comes up," and then discipline yourself to act accordingly. Many people find that their most creative moments revolve around sleep time, (i.e. just before retiring, upon arising or in the middle of the night) when intuition is "closest to the surface." So review your notes or business papers right before you go to sleep and let your subconscious have at it. Keep paper and pencil (or tape recorder) on your nightstand so you can record your flashes of insight when they occur.

Fortunately, the more success we experience in using our intuitive power, the more we will be inclined to use it. As ol' uncle Ollie used to say: "The antidote to self-doubt is success." Keep in mind the examples of success cited earlier and the endorsement of Albert Einstein: "I could not have arrived at my understanding of the laws of the universe through my rational mind alone."

Eventually, our own successes will build our confidence in our intuitive strengths. But first, we must let the genie out of the bottle. Psychologists tell us that this feat depends on our ability to create circumstances that will serve to release our intuitive riches from the closet of our subconscious and put to work our most underutilized personal precocity.

While intuition should not totally supplant other, more deliberate, analytical forms of decision making, it can be used as a very potent supplement, one that can give your firm a critical edge over its left-brain driven competitors. Indeed, a study by psychologists at the Universities of Virginia and Pittsburgh concluded that people who listen to their intuition and don't analyze their decisions in depth often make better choices, at least about their own lives.

DOUBLE YOUR FAILURES

From error to error, one discovers the entire truth.

—Sigmund Freud, Psychiatrist

"The secret to success is to double your failure rate." That was the belief of Thomas Watson Jr., the legendary president of IBM.

Q. I just read an article on "failure" that suggested making mistakes in business could be a positive trait. How do you explain this?

A. A business leader who never fails is not experimenting, risking and innovating sufficiently. Uninterrupted success bespeaks performance at a level less than could be achieved if one took a few chances and really pushed his or her talents to the limit. Truly significant success can only be achieved by a person who occasionally fails because that person is reaching, striving and accomplishing in ways that stretch his abilities beyond the "fail-safe" point.

Nevertheless, we are a society so obsessed with success that we are, by and large, blind to the value of failure. Duped by the macho musings of Vince Lombardi, we tend to believe that "winning is the only thing." We've lost sight of Henry Ford's sage observation: "Failure is the opportunity to begin......more intelligently."

A successful achiever readily acknowledges, deals with, and purposefully recovers from failure when it occurs. Wilson Kemmons, the founder of Holiday Inn, once said: "My own success was attended by quite a few failures along the way. But I refused to make the biggest mistake of all: worrying too much about making mistakes. A man who never makes mistakes, never does anything. I have made as many or more mistakes than most people, but I always try to learn from them and to profit from my failures."

Charles Kettering, the inventor of the automobile self-starter, believed that it was not a disgrace to fail as long as one sought to understand its cause. He believed that "failing intelligently" was "one of the greatest arts in the world." Kettering offered a prescription for turning failure into success: "1) Honestly face defeat, never fake success; 2) Exploit the failure, don't waste it. Learn all you can from it; 3) Never use failure as an excuse for not trying again."

Admitting to a failure and quickly moving to deal with its origins and impacts is absolutely essential. President Richard Nixon was a classic example of a leader who continually denied his personal failings, thus allowing them to metastasize into an unredeemable defeat of gigantic proportions.

However, since most of the values imparted to us at home and in school during our formative years focus on making us winners, it is difficult for us to acknowledge our failures. Ironically, most of what we actually do in life could be easily rated "less than successful." Batting .400 is an outstanding achievement.

Even batting .100 is worthwhile, because trial and error is the way we learn. Investigation of our failings typically produces discoveries that constitute better, and frequently successful, new beginnings.

Only by accepting the possibility of failure and by seeing that failure as a respectable learning experience, will we be strong enough to manifest the bold, experimental and achievement-oriented behavior that is required of leaders in today's rapidly changing world.

Occasional failures are a natural outgrowth of simply trying your best. They are inevitable milestones of perseverance on any path of personal progress. Permanent, debilitating failure will only occur when you quit trying.

Successful owners and managers know that they can more quickly produce more value, by stretching, making a mistake, and correcting it, than they can by limiting themselves to totally risk-less undertakings.

Steve Roth, the creator of the Time Warner behemoth, said that, in his company, "people get fired for <u>not</u> making mistakes."

Brass Tacks Tip: Accept your own failures and be tolerant of the "nonsuccess" of your followers. To do this, you have to nurture an organizational culture that openly allows for failure. Your followers will not tap their intuitive, innovative, risk-taking talents if they believe that failure is unacceptable. Consequently, you must make your followers feel that there will be no unwarranted retribution as a consequence of failures encountered in the course of sincere, well-intentioned, industrious effort.

Of course, once occurring, each such miscarriage should be evaluated, analyzed and understood so that it will not recur and so that another, more successful effort can be launched in its wake. Failures represent a cost, so you and your followers are obliged to ensure that each "investment" in failure has a good prospect for producing a future positive return. Let your team members know that you embrace Confucius' observation: "True accomplishment is not in never failing, but in rising again after you fall."

To provide your followers with the security they need to wholeheartedly accept such a philosophy, you'll have to help them see that "participative failure" in the context of the mission of the enterprise doesn't necessarily indicate the kind of personal failure that is bred of individual shortcomings. The personalization of failure can cause great harm to both the afflicted employee and the enterprise as a whole. Indeed, most failures within an organization cannot be reasonably attributed to a single individual. There are many direct and indirect, present and historical, and situational and cultural influences that condition the potential for individual success and failure within an enterprise.

It's also important to keep in mind that everything we do should not be weighed on a simple two-stop meter of "success" and "failure." Former Vice President Dan Quayle was off the mark when he opined: "If we do not succeed, then we run the risk of failure." Most of what we do falls into a "neutral zone," a dimension in which we toil, without obvious victory, to learn and test the things that hopefully will bring us to ultimate, future success. My ol' uncle Ollie used to say: "Failing to succeed is just one step on the path to success."

TAKE THE LEAD

I must follow the people. Am I not their leader?

—Benjamin Disraeli, Statesman and Novelist

According to my ol' uncle Ollie, "leaders are not born, they are self-conceived."

Q. I read a lot about the importance of leadership but have never seen it succinctly defined. In your opinion, what is a leader and what do you have to do to be a good one?

A. A leader is a person who is wise enough to share meaningful insights, strong enough to share the power to pursue those insights, brave enough to let others exploit the opportunity, and generous enough to share the rewards of accomplishment. While other definitions abound, two of the best have come from academicians familiar with the process of leadership development. Harvard Professor Rosabeth Ross Kanter suggests that leadership is "the art of mastering change......the ability to mobilize others' efforts in new directions." Tom Gerrity, Dean of the Wharton School, claims that "leadership is the ability to inspire and develop others......to bring forth their fullest potential and highest capabilities......to encourage them to accomplish a mission as a team."

President Truman had an equally telling, if slightly more cynical, definition. A leader, he said, "has the ability to get other people to do what they don't want to do and like it."

Another President, Theodore Roosevelt, believed "the best executive is the one who has enough sense to pick good men (and women) to do what he wants done and self-restraint enough to keep from meddling with them while they do it."

These definitions suggest that leadership is a social process in which the numero uno points the way and then uses his or her personal ability, charisma, trust, example and communication to take others along on an important mission. In the process, he or she inspires and motivates followers to contribute the best they have to the successful completion of that mission.

All of this suggests an even simpler definition: Leaders are people who muster and motivate good followers. With respect to his or her followers, a good leader:

• Collectively identifies—<u>with</u> his or her followers—worthwhile goals for change and achievement.

• Knows them intimately—their insights, talents, experience, biases, fears and aspirations.

• Explains the goals of the enterprise in a way that inspires them to wholeheartedly cooperate in their attainment.

• Challenges them to accomplishment and creates an environment in which their efforts will produce stimulation and satisfaction for them.

• Gives them the perspective to appreciate the unique aptitudes they bring to the performance equation.

• Helps them organize, apply and continually refresh their personal abilities in a way that brings forth their best work.

• Provides the kind of tangible and intangible assistance that reinforces and magnifies the personal force they bring to their tasks.

• Shares with them the knowledge, experience and authority they need to get the job done.

- Maintains an environment that encourages them to share, innovate, experiment, take risk and accept the possibility of failure.

- Provides a personal example of the kind of commitment, industriousness and contributory behavior that you want them to emulate.

- Communicates with them in a manner that provides unfettered feedback concerning their mission and their personal contributions to its accomplishment.

- Assists them in understanding and overcoming the personal and organizational conflicts, resistance, fears and confusion that can encumber their efforts.

- Protects them from the bureaucratic nonsense that plagues every organization that has more than one member.

- Is readily available to them to provide redirection when appropriate.

- Provides meaningful recognition, appreciation and approbation for jobs well done.

Brass Tacks Tip: In the final analysis, it will be your followers who will make you a good leader. In this respect, Ghandi's very simple definition of leadership takes center stage. "Leaders," he said, "are people who find out where the parade is going and get in front of it." An apt and accurate observation…if you've got good, motivated marchers moving in the right direction.

Good followers can produce great leaders. But it is up to a leader to create such followership. Robert Townsend, a writer and former CEO of Avis Rent-A-Car, claimed that "the real essence of leadership is to care about your people, to help them get as much as they can out of the business environment and to have as much fun as they can. Anybody who can do that—and really mean it—is a leader."

BELIEVE AND ACHIEVE

Do not follow the ideas of others, but learn to listen to the voice within yourself.

—Dogen, Japanese religious leader

"It ain't braggin' if you can do it." Mohammed Ali's ability to put his supreme confidence in perspective offers a lesson for all of us.

Q. In a previous column you emphasized that a good leader needs to be self-confident. I've always believed that a big ego is a dangerous thing. Don't you think you overdid it?

A. No. I've long adhered to Samuel Johnson's observation: "Self-confidence is the first requisite to great undertakings." Indeed, experience has taught me that to function entrepreneurially—in your own business or in somebody else's—you need a great degree of self-confidence. In his book, The Alexander Complex, Michael Meyer states that the people who can make a real difference in a business enterprise "live in the grip of a vision. Work and career take on the quality of a mission, a pursuit of some Holy Grail. And, because they are talented and convinced they can change the world, they often do."

Interestingly, one-in-three classic entrepreneurs rank their success potential at the start of a new venture as a 10 on a scale of 10! They believe, like the consummate, eccentric entrepreneur Howard Hughes, that "if it can be conceived, it can be built."

In the words of Thomas Duck Sr., founder of the Ugly Duckling Rent-a-Car System and veteran of more than two dozen different occupations: "I always felt I could fly......if I just moved my arms properly!!"

Truly successful business owners and managers love to be confronted with the conclusion that "it can't be done." That's all the stimulation they need to set out to prove the contrary.

In psychological terms, these people enjoy an inner drive; an internal "locus of control." This inner drive to accomplish and attain......to succeed......prompts them to march to their own "inner drum," no matter what it requires or how long it will take. These individuals enjoy a sense of destiny derived from an inner conviction. This assurance results from a sensitivity to self, rather than to the influence of external factors like other people and events. They are confident and optimistic about the future. Their self-concept is that of "rugged individualist." Important is their feeling that their personal destinies and those of their firms are conditioned primarily by factors that are—or can be—under their control, influenced by a power that emanates from within them.

These achievers believe that they control their life and that "externals" exert little influence. The "locus of control" is within them. They really believe that they can walk on hot rocks without getting blisters.

To be a real "doer," you can't just TRY to make things happen. According to the book High Impact Skills for Your Success, underachievers use the word TRY an average of eight times a day compared with high achievers who say try only once a day.

This sense of personal, active control is different from the passive anxiety control that is employed by many people who are not self-confident and proactive in their affairs. Passive individuals generally try to accommodate existing realities to reduce their anxieties. They try to become part of a larger group, to bend with the wind, to rationalize events to see a bright side, to put themselves in the hands of "the fates." (Some observers claim that this trait among many Japanese managers is a major reason why that nation's innovation rate falls far behind that of the United States.)

Effective leaders, on the other hand, exercise <u>active</u> anxiety control. They welcome the feelings of apprehension that inevitably accompany change. They trust themselves and don't reflexively "join the crowd." They suspend judgment and look at things as an inquisitive scientist would, reaching out to proactively discover and act.

Brass Tacks Tip: To realize the most from this kind of behavior you have to cultivate a very keen awareness of your surroundings and the things that are happening externally. It's important to feel at liberty to act according to your feelings and senses. Spontaneity is vital. Moreover, you can't allow yourself to be embarrassed by your enthusiasm or be bridled by conventionality.

Kemmons Wilson, the founder of Holiday Inn, demonstrated these traits. On a car trip in the early 1950's, he lamented the lack of motel accommodations that were family-friendly; and he was convinced he could profit from it despite his wife's amused incredulity. He was convinced, he told her, that "we could build a better motel chain that would eventually number as many as 400 units." He knew he could do it; and he was committed to doing it. When he retired 28 years later, there were 1,759 Holiday Inns.

Whenever I think of confidence and dedication to task, I recall the amazing accomplishment of Jean-Dominique Bauby, who was the high-living editor of <u>Elle</u> magazine. At age forty-four, he suffered a devastating stroke which left him "locked in" his body, unable to move. Eighteen months later he began work on a moving memoir, <u>The Diving Bell and the Butterfly</u>. He achieved it despite near total paralysis by moving his left eyelid to select letters he wished to use as another person read the alphabet. If, at some point in your adventures, you feel self-confidence is a vice, just read his work.

HIRE RIGHT

Hiring the first employee is, arguably, the most significant step an entrepreneur takes during the course of his or her venture.

Q. After years of leading a "one man band," I am about to hire an assistant to help me run and, hopefully, expand this business. Frankly, the whole idea makes me nervous. Any advice???

A. Even in large organizations, it is essential to have enough talent on board to optimize worthwhile opportunities to expand and develop. Your prudent admission that you can't do everything yourself—forever—marks the beginning of a new and very different way of doing business that should pay handsome rewards down the line.

However, while this step will greatly advance your efforts to get the highest and best return from your enterprise, it will also require you to "let go" and delegate some of the authority and responsibility—and rewards—that previously were yours alone. To empower others who will "certainly not do it as well as you could" is always difficult for a Type A, *"have it my way"* kind of person. But there's really no other choice. Indeed, many firms fail because they default on growth opportunities that more flexible and daring competitors are willing to seize. Just keep in mind, a proper handing-off of duties will free you up to tackle the issues that you can address better than anyone.

Of course, there will be risk. But if you select and prepare your followers carefully, and "give them their head," they will, in most cases, do it well enough. And they will learn, improve, and grow in reliable capacity. Odds are, your new hire will eventually produce valuable ideas and approaches that your proven "experience" might not have allowed you to fashion yourself.

There are a few important *Brass Tacks Tips* that you should keep in mind as you hire your first employee and as you continue to build your workforce:

- Always start with good people. Take the time to hire the best you can afford. Every time you hire someone, evaluate his or her potential for someday doing your job, and doing it better than you do. My ol' uncle Ollie used to say: "First rate people hire first rate people; Third-rate people hire second rate people."

- Make sure the duties you are delegating are sufficiently broad to allow the person to be challenged by them to explore, improvise and innovate as he or she implements. With such latitude he will, in all probability, generate benefits far beyond those that would be achieved if he were told exactly what to do.

- Develop an intimate understanding of your new follower's abilities, both extant and potential. In some cases it will require you to provide advance training or preparation. One of the major reasons that Hitler was defeated in World War II was his inability to acknowledge the competence of his experienced generals.

- Test the limits. Always try to give an employee a tad more responsibility than he feels he can handily carry. It will stretch him and take him—and you—to new levels of performance.

- Enter into a formal compact with your new follower that outlines the challenge you are delegating. This "contract" should spell out the authority and responsibility that is being transferred; it should delineate ambitions expectations; and, it should be in writing. Both parties to the delegation process must fully understand its implications—before execution—and they must both formally sign-off on it, so that each can be appropriately measured by the outcomes this relationship produces.

- Take it in steps if you are unsure about a person's capacity for accepting new responsibilities. You can gauge—and help develop—their abilities by giving them responsibility in degrees. Start out by telling him to "formulate a recommendation for my approval." Eventually, you want to be able to say: "Make a decision and implement it. No need to check with me."

- Be sure the person assuming the responsibility has a clear appreciation of the benefits and rewards that will accrue to him as a consequence of good performance. In fact, you should convey an expectation that the final rewards can actually exceed those initially envisioned, if outcomes exceed those that were initially agreed to. Such open-ended "personal profit potential" will instill a sense of "ownership" in the mission and can inspire some very beneficial "entrepreneurial" behavior.

- Establish a non-intrusive, informal system of communication that will afford you the essential feedback you require to monitor progress. You want just enough information to determine if some prudent counseling, support or resources could be put to good use. Err on the side of not knowing. If you've got a good person doing the job, ignorance can be bliss.

- Carefully measure the help you provide as he proceeds. Too much "hand-holding" will stifle his creativity; too little can hobble his progress. The wisest course is to give him just enough to get started. Then stand ready to provide help when it's asked for. He's got to know it's his job to do.

Through this whole process, remember that your job as leader is to duplicate yourself in others. You want people to rise to your level of competence, pushing you upward and forward in the process. As my ol' uncle Ollie used to say, "Keeping good people down, ain't the way to stay on top."

DEVELOP GREAT FOLLOWERS

There is something much more scarce and rarer than ability. It is the ability to recognize ability.

—Robert Half, Businessman

Of necessity, any worthwhile definition of "leadership" must include the important component of "followership."

Q. I agree with your definition of leadership, but I don't think you paid enough attention to the "followers" that every manager must rely on. Don't you agree that developing good followers and getting rid of the bad is my number one job as an operator of a business?

A. In the hustle and bustle of daily business, managers frequently fail to appreciate that a leader can be only as good as those who follow him or her......that the true measure of a leader is the followership he or she creates. Indeed, the personal and professional success of a leader ultimately depends upon the achievements of those they empower and energize. John D. Rockefeller clearly let his managers know what was important to him. He proclaimed: "I will pay more for the ability to deal with people than for any other ability under the sun."

One of the most important duties of a manager is to instill in his team members a strong belief in their own abilities. Followers must be convinced that they have the personal capacity and know-how to accomplish their mission. They must truly believe that they have the talent to achieve the task at hand come hell or high water. Accordingly, you have to continuously strive to positively reinforce each follower's self-concept and sense of destiny.

Baseball legend Reggie Jackson succinctly defined what it takes: "I'll tell you what makes a great manager: a great manager has a knack for making ballplayers think they are better than they think they are. He forces you to have a good opinion of yourself. He lets you know he believes in you. He makes you get more out of yourself. And once you learn how good you really are, you never settle for playing anything less than your very best."

The best leader is a transparent leader. Followers will be aggressive—and successful—in their undertakings if they believe that it is their personal conviction, commitment and contribution that makes the difference. Philosopher Lea-Tse described the important, invisible influence of a leader this way: "A leader is best when people barely know he exists. Not so good when people obey and acclaim him. Worse when they despise him. But of a good leader, who talks little......when his work is done, his aim fulfilled......the people will say: 'We did it ourselves'."

Notwithstanding all of the above, experience shows that some followers simply cannot make the grade. Therefore, it is up to the leader to have a sufficiently acute understanding of his charges so that he can ultimately determine who, after all of his ministrations, should make the final cut. Building a team with strong players at every position is one of the principal responsibilities of a leader. He or she must find the "weak links" and either make them strong or make them leave, and perform this delicate triage judiciously, compassionately and quickly.

Author and educator Robert E. Kelley of Carnegie Mellon University constructed a simple model—featuring intersecting axes creating four quadrants—to help leaders screen their followers and take appropriate team-building action. Using this model, he divides followers into camps of "independent critical-thinkers" or "dependent uncritical thinkers" (on the opposite ends of the north-south axis); and into "active" or "passive" participants (on the extremes of the east-west axis). The passive-dependent followers (in the southwest quadrant) he calls "sheep" since they don't think for themselves and will do whatever they are asked to do even if it is wrong. They are generally slow and unenthusiastic.

The active, uncritical thinkers in an organization's southeast quarter will respond aggressively to direction given by the leader but are loath to evaluate or criticize. Kelley calls these folks "YES" people, while many of their colleagues are inclined to tab them "suck-ups." (Interestingly, weak, unenlightened managers are inclined to see them as "most accommodating" and generally favor them at promotion time. They find that "clones are comfortable," a career-killing conviction at best.)

In time, with education, support and the proper incentives, the people in these two quadrants can be developed into reasonable, if marginally productive, followers.

Of course the most productive, effective followers—the organization's future leaders—are those who are active and independent. These critical thinkers reside in the northeast quadrant. They are the hard-to-handle PITA's (pains in the anatomy) who have their own ideas and agendas and are extremely vocal about them. They question everything, but will give a leader incredible performance if they are given a challenging task, adequate tools and ample leeway. They'll make their leader and their organization great if they are offered appropriate respect, responses and rewards.

The dregs of the lot are the independent, passive critical thinkers. They're bright, Kelley says, but they keep their thoughts to themselves. These counter-productive subversives (in the southwest corner of the model) are not on the team and are pleased to see the leader stumble and fail, even if they could act to avoid it. According to Kelley, they are unredeemable enemies who have to be purged from the system as quickly as possible.

Kurt Wiedenhaupt, the former CEO of American Precision Industries, draws similar quadrants basing the north-south axis on intelligence and the east-west line on effort. He claims the dumb-and-lazy are a drag and the smart-and-lazy "are the death knell for a company. "A good leader," he claims, "will jettison both as soon as possible while forging energetic, entrepreneurial people of any intelligence level into effective followers."

Your goal is to unleash your obstreperous, effective followers and upgrade your "YES" people to critical thinkers and doers.

It's not an easy job but, then, as Reuben Mark, a former CEO of Colgate Palmolive, once observed: "In the final analysis, it's not the general who wins, but the army."

KEEP THE GOOD ONES

Friendship is like money, easier made than kept.

—Samuel Butler, Writer and Poet

The backbone of any business is a cadre of talented, industrious employees. Accordingly, defections by key employees can break the back of an enterprise.

Q. I own and operate a small business that depends on well-trained workers. Nowadays, I feel like I'm running a vocational training school for larger, more well-heeled companies in my area. As soon as I get a worker trained and up to speed—and begin reaping the fruits of my training efforts—POOF! A bigger, more cash-flush firm steals him away. I react quickly to any discontent, but still the churning continues. What can I do to stem this outflow of my most important resource?

A. Unfortunately, poaching of this type has become pretty routine and even a downturn in the economy probably won't quell it. Why? Because the understandable goal of every enterprise struggling in today's competitive world is to get and keep the best of the best. In a way, it's sort of a backhanded compliment to your abilities as a developer of talent. Now you have to focus on your responsibilities as a "keeper" of talent.

Years ago, sociologist Frederick Herzberg postulated the "Hygiene/ Motivation Theory" when analyzing what could be done in a company's internal environment to motivate good workers. I believe it also will help you see what must be done to <u>keep</u> the talented employees you have.

The hygiene part of his approach involved "cleansing" the workplace of negatives that were clear turnoffs to workers, thus allowing them to feel, at best, neutral about their circumstances. He claimed that this was accomplished by providing adequate supervision, a good, "clean" working environment, maintaining effective interpersonal relations, and offering competitive salaries, status, and security. Note, however, that these "essentials" will only get you to ground zero, a state in which you have "conditioned" the workplace to eliminate dissatisfaction. While these elements are necessary in every situation, in order to truly motivate—and keep—the best employees, Herzberg's theory suggests you have to go much further. Here is where your abilities as a motivator come into play.

You must continually strive to enhance that which your employees <u>do</u> in order to increase their sense of personal achievement. This will, in turn, enhance their proclivity to stay where that invaluable feeling of personal accomplishment is ever-present. Effective leaders—I call them *MetaManagers*®—have to enable their followers to gain a sense of achievement by structuring their responsibilities in a way that presents a meaningful challenge and a true sense of personal and professional accomplishment. This means giving them increasingly expanded responsibilities and the freedom and authority to execute them independently. The best way to keep a crewmember on board is to let him or her enjoy a sense of personal growth and advancement....and to be personally recognized for that accomplishment.

Here are a few additional ***Brass Tacks Tips:*** for creating this kind of "retentive" environment:

- Hire the right workers in the first place. You want a workforce that shares your entrepreneurial zeal and penchant for hard work. These predispositions can be determined through simple tests administered as part of the pre-hiring interview process. Continually work to build your knowledge of every employee after they are hired, too. Your personal leadership activities must be tailored to the many unique facets of the special workforce you build.

- Create a culture that ambitious people can buy into. Ensure that your business model promises success, both collectively and individually. The environment you maintain should support the values, ethics and aspirations of your colleagues. Work diligently to promulgate an understanding of this culture.

- Make sure each team member has meaningful work to do. This means you have to be creative in structuring the nature of the work each person does. Boredom or a sense that an employee is doing something beneath his or her abilities is a "turn off" that is sure to "turn out" talent. A good job description will stipulate what must be done to ensure adequate company performance, but it must also take into consideration what the worker implementing it needs in order to gain a sense of personal performance. This means that a job must be continually enlarged, enhanced and embellished in order to keep an employee satisfactorily engaged.

- Delegate and empower. Don't knit-pick and hover over your charges. Trust them to do a good job. This will be tough for a hands-on entrepreneur like you, but really talented employees need a mentor, not a boss. They should feel like they work "with" you, not "for" you. Of course, to make this work, they have to understand the goals of your firm and, ideally, participate in formulating them.

- Provide the tools, technology and personal example necessary for them to do a good job. Your team must know you are committed to winning. Set the example. "Walk the walk" and they will follow.

- Show each team member that he or she makes a big, unique difference. Public approbation and recognition are essential. (Consider what generals accomplish with colored ribbon!) Offer immediate, positive, personal feedback when a job is done well.

- Compensate creatively. Competitive salaries and benefits are merely hygiene factors that keep an employee from harboring negative feelings. To bring out the "gusto," you will have to consider benefits that recognize a follower's "specialness." This requires a thorough understanding of each employee's hot buttons. Consider a "cafeteria" type benefit plan that covers everything from flextime options to stock options (although I prefer "virtual equity" to actual equity ownership in small businesses). Think about "golden handcuffs"—benefits that kick in over time—to continually reward loyalty and promote tenure.

- Conduct exit interviews with departing workers. The best maintenance policies are predicated on an understanding of why things break. Also, make sure to give special attention to those who remain when an employee leaves, nurturing an accurate appreciation of the reasons why the co-worker has departed. Work quickly with the colleagues of the departed to diffuse any temptation to follow.

- Give everyone a chance to grow, learn and enhance his or her personal value. On-the-job training and off-site educational opportunities increase an employee's sense of self-esteem and self-worth. Most workers know that 70 percent of the jobs they will be doing in ten years are unknown today. Help them get ready for the future and you have a good chance of keeping them with you as it unfolds.

COUNT ON YOURSELF

If you can find a mission in life worth working for—and if you believe in yourself—nothing can stop you from achieving success.

—Kemmons Wilson, Founder of Holiday Inn

To modify a famous Trumanism, the buck STARTS with a firm's CEO......its Chief Entrepreneurial Officer. As a consequence, that person has to be perpetually "pumped" to master the many tasks at hand.

Q. I run a company with almost three hundred employees. I'm trying to make some important changes, but help from the managers and employees who work for me is mighty scarce. How do I get these folks to be more cooperative? This shouldn't be a one-man band.

A. Don't turn in your kazoo. Both corporate leaders and bandleaders typically suffer solitary, unshared responsibility. Keep in mind that you—and you alone—are responsible for creating a compelling vision, orchestrating meaningful participation, inspiring extraordinary contributions and appropriately rewarding those who help you accomplish the mission.

Naturally, you can't do everything yourself, but before you can entreat your followers for assistance, you must look to your own personal orientation, attitudes and proclivities to ensure that they are primed for the task at hand. Such a self-analysis has to be penetrating and honest, and it must focus on the internal strengths that you can personally muster.

While adequate capital, systems, equipment, and a competent and willing workforce <u>add</u> to the propelling vim and verve of an enterprise, the driving force of change must be conceived, energized and directed by the leader as an individual. Organizational resources are always important to the task of implementation, but it is the leader—*solely*—who is responsible for initiating, nurturing and guiding all change-making activity.

Indeed, in today's world, where cost-cutting, downsizing and "re-engineering" are de rigueur, managers are finding that they frequently have to "fly solo," without a lot of the organizational support that was available in days gone by. No longer can you depend on having elaborate organizations of people and extensive resources at your beck and call. These days, most managers are being asked to do more with less, to function more like guerrillas who must plan their own attacks, draw their own maps, recruit supporters along the way and adjust their tactics as they move. When it comes to material support, they must find and forage, and earn their support through worthy accomplishment.

This type of performance requires a strong, burning entrepreneurial desire to accomplish. In his 1961 book, <u>The Achieving Society</u>, Harvard social psychologist David C. McClelland tells us that people are motivated by three principal needs. The proportions in which these needs propel us tend to determine our capacity for success as entrepreneurial personalities. In other words, the needs you accede to have a lot to say about your capacity for the kind of behavior essential to leading change in modern corporations.

The three needs defined my McClelland are the need for power, the need for affiliation and the need for achievement.

Persons with power needs feel they must influence others and are very concerned about how they are perceived by others. Reputation and status are extremely important to them. As a consequence, they tend to take forceful actions that impact others and they generally try to gain control over people by regulating their behavior. These folks tend to arouse emotional feelings and reactions both as a means of achieving dominance and as a result of their actions. They tend to make good policemen or drill sergeants but not bosses of contemporary corporations.

Individuals with a need for affiliation strive to build warm relationships. Friendships are critical to them. They are very attracted to social situations and commonly exhibit deep concern for other people. They do not like to be separated, in any way, from people with whom they have relationships, and they make special efforts to be liked. Teachers, personnel specialists, nurses and social workers generally are motivated by affiliation needs.

Those with a need for achievement have to excel at everything they do, especially projects that are unique or extremely demanding. They strive to do well at every task they undertake, and they like to have their performance measured. They work to surpass self-imposed standards. They do not need taskmasters; they are adept at "firing their own starting gun." As a consequence, they seek honest and meaningful feedback. These people generally formulate long-term goals and plans that are particularly sensitive to the need to overcome obstacles. Needless to say, these people make good entrepreneurs. Their example, commitment and willingness to work hard also energize those around them. These are the folks that others want to help; they naturally inspire those around them.

Brass Tacks Tip: To be an effective leader you must be—and be seen as—an achiever, a self-motivated driver with a personal commitment to success. This is the only way you'll get others to enthusiastically contribute to your target achievement.

The renowned chronicler of the entrepreneurial spirit, Joseph Schumpeter, aptly described the personality you have to emulate: "There is the dream and the will......there is the will to conquer; the impulse to fight, to prove oneself......to succeed for the sake of—not the fruits of—success itself. Finally, there is the joy of creating, of getting things done, of simply exercising one's energy and imagination."

Is this you?? An impresario with these traits can lead his or her band anywhere.

BE UNPROFESSIONAL

Doing something right is not as rewarding as doing the right things.

—Ol' Uncle Ollie, Relative

It's possible that the term "management professional" is an oxymoron.

Q. My brother, the dentist, claims that as a business like mine matures, I must become more of a professional manager than an entrepreneur. Is he right?

A. Not in my book. By definition, a profession is a calling requiring specialized knowledge and long and intensive preparation including instruction in skills and methods as well as in the scientific, historical or scholarly principles underlying those skills and methods. Facts, numbers, systems, routines, procedures and methodologies are the fodder of professionals.

In The Principles of Scientific Management, Frederick Winslow Taylor endeavored to prove that "the best management is a true science, resting upon clearly defined laws." To wit, if a person knows the laws, he or she has what it takes to be successful.

For most of the twentieth century, it was believed by business managers—and the schools that produced them—that if a person knew the analytical routines, had the right numbers, and commanded enough drones to execute his divine, calculated conclusions, good results would naturally be forthcoming. The importance of the human factor, luck, the art of energizing people and organizations, and the ability to reflexively exploit change as it happens were downplayed.

If we are to believe this old construct, a navigator could qualify as a professional; an explorer probably would not. Yet, it is the motivated, curious, ingenious, avaricious, exploitative explorers who build great businesses, not the "navigators" who primarily serve as the plotters of other peoples' desired courses.

In recent years, we've seen what can happen to companies managed by "suits" who go strictly by the book. The unfortunate collisions with reality suffered by the likes of Kodak, Westinghouse, Xerox, Kmart, Montgomery Ward and Chrysler, have prompted corporate shareholders, and the directors who speak for them, to conclude that today's business leaders, in order to be effective, must transcend the structured scientific paths of "professionalism" to the art of leadership. We now understand that executives must move beyond the rigid principles that are the foundations of most professions and, instead, master the less precise arts of creativity, innovation, visioning, exploitation, risk-taking and doing the impossible.

For ninety-six percent of the past two millennia, most economic progress was forged individually by adventurers and venturers. Solitary farmers, foragers, craftsmen and traders worked to deliver products and services directly to individual consumers. An "entrepreneurial" model of resource mobilization prevailed.

As we entered the industrial era, however, mass production began to find mass markets and this simple model changed. Gradually, entrepreneurs and capital providers began to see that great benefits could be derived from division of labor, economies of scale, and formal organizational structures that were "administered" by a new class of managers.

By the 1920's, Alfred Sloan, the head of General Motors, formally recognized this new class of managers, recognizing them as "professionals." (He's the same guy that once said: "It is impossible to reach the conclusion that (foreign) motor cars......could be produced and sold in competition in the American market.") This new stratum of non-owner operators, which had initially emerged as a supplement to the entrepreneurial geniuses who had actually created enterprises, eventually began to supplant them. At the time, this evolution seemed to make sense, especially to capital-providers who were increasingly called upon to invest in corporate ventures. "Managers" facilitated the growth and diversification that were hallmarks of the maturing industrial era.

Not all observers of this phenomenon were sanguine. In his book, The New Industrial State, John Kenneth Galbraith lamented the emergence of what he referred to as a "technostructure" that "replaces the entrepreneur as the directing force of the enterprise with management" and runs corporations in the interests of those management caretakers.

But economic society's love affair with management continued until the 1980's. The high-water mark in the corporate management power trip came with the introduction of the conglomerate in the 1960's and 70's. These penultimate grabs for size and random diversification were rationalized by virtue of managers' declared abilities to analyze, control and create profits "by the numbers." Middle managers, supervisors and line workers were seen as mere "implementers" who could perform miracles at the behest of senior management if they were programmed properly, pointed in the right direction, and given the numbers they were to follow and the numbers they were to produce. It was believed that if a CEO were smart enough, he or she could analyze, organize and direct almost any form of endeavor on almost any scale. Folks like Royal Little (Textron), Harold Geneen (ITT), and James Ling (LTV) were a few of the most ambitious "conglomerateers" who set a pattern that many other full-of-themselves managers would emulate. Alas, only a few, like Jack Welch at GE, succeeded over the long term.

Ultimately, by the 1980's, a number of Kryptonite-like forces conspired to deflate and defeat these high-flying supermanagers. One by one, these lunges at size and conglomeration unraveled. Global competition; rampant innovation; an explosion in information and the techniques to use it; the emergence of more able, vocal and independent stakeholders; and the acceleration of change in every marketplace demonstrated the accumulated weaknesses of the "super management" model. Author Robert Samuelson observed: "With bigger bureaucracies, companies couldn't respond quickly to market changes, new technologies, competitors or customer needs. The more powerful top executives became, the less they knew. Their information was filtered through staff reports and statistical tables."

Many large corporations, including those cited earlier, began to realize that the key to survival and success in the new millennium was a return to the entrepreneurial vigor, industriousness, and vision that made these enterprises great in the first place. They wisely concluded that they needed innovative, risk-taking, change-making entrepreneurial leaders who could go beyond the narrowly defined prescripts and precepts of traditional "professionalism"......the kinds of "meta-professionals" who could make contemporary enterprises fast, flexible and ferocious enough to stay in the game and win.

Brass Tacks Tip: Remind your brother that Mike Tyson was long considered a "professional" boxer.

SEEK LEADERS EVERYWHERE

Big shots are only little shots who keep shooting.

—Christopher Morley, Writer

When it comes to leadership styles, it cannot be said that "one size fits all." Leaders emerge from different backgrounds, favor distinctive approaches, enjoy varying degrees of charisma and play various roles in an organization.

Q. I have only a few good leaders in my firm. In your opinion, where should I place them to do the most good for my company?

A. Leadership is important in every corner of an enterprise.

Most leaders are best categorized according to their responsibilities. All companies have four fundamental dimensional realms in which they operate: internal and external; present and future. Envision four compass points. North=a firm's external dimension, its markets and the world in which it must function; South=its internal space, the plant and facilities in which its marketable values are produced; West=the present; East=the future. Draw two lines, one connecting North and South, the other joining East and West. The lower left quadrant so produced is where "operational leadership" flourishes. The diagonally opposite, upper right quadrant is the realm in which "directional leadership" is essential.

"Operational leaders" concentrate on the methods a firm employs to manufacture value. They look inward to here-and-now concerns. The efficacy of the systems, capital, and technology employed by the company is their primary concern. They strive to reduce resource consumption and to produce quality goods or services at low cost. Here, traditional management talents can be put to good use. Process control, manufacturing, organization, staffing and purchasing are key issues of concern. The "stuff" that one learns in business school, coupled with an ability to work with and through people, is put to good use in this realm. Technical and human skills are primary requisites.

Begging a military analogy, these folks are behind the lines doing yeoman's work in the Quartermaster's Corps. They provide the critical wherewithal that will be employed by the maneuver elements in the battlefield. Without the resources and support provided here, no successful engagement of the enemy can occur. After all, it has been said "every army travels on its stomach."

Of course, one of the primary goals of an enterprise—or an army—is to reduce the number of leaders and followers employed in these kinds of activities, freeing up as many combatants as possible for front line duty. A leader's abilities to introduce improved technology and increase productivity make a big difference here. Speed, simplification, efficiency, productivity and cost reduction are paramount.

But victory also depends upon equally sound leadership in the external/future (northeast) quadrant of an enterprise's activity, where nontraditional, entrepreneurial management skills are most valuable. It is there that the "pathfinder's" directional leadership determines where the enterprise is going and how successful—vis-à-vis the competition—it will be in its journey.

It is in this realm in which leaders concentrate on the outside world and on the pursuit of a winning direction. It is here that an enterprise can build an unmatched and enduring advantage. This is where the entrepreneurial, creative, innovative talents of a leader can make the crucial competitive difference. Here the "infantry" uses all of its ingenuity, courage and guile to out-maneuver, out-shoot and outsmart the enemy in real time. This is where the strength of the firm, as forged by its "operational leadership," is applied by its "directional leadership" in the pursuit of victory.

Brass Tacks Tip: There can be heroes in every quadrant of your firm's endeavor. The externally focused leader is not necessarily more important than the leader who is dedicated to internal affairs. However, these days, we are discovering that there is an acute shortage of leaders who can function well in the external/future quadrant. That's because the bulk of today's management cadres have been trained in schools and have had their experiences honed in enterprises that are not externally sensitized, not entrepreneurially driven. As a consequence, too much of a firm's capacity is engaged in the continued pursuit and production of what was or is, and too little is devoted to what the external environments of the enterprise will demand in the short and long term future.

The consequences of failure to look outward, beyond the present, can be very costly. A good example is the opportunities lost by Xerox Corp. A decade before the advent of the PC, Xerox's Palo Alto research center had developed, internally, all of the critical elements of the personal computer, from the mouse to the laser printer. In the early 1970's, Xerox researchers had developed cascading windows and icons and put all those features together in a device that looks remarkably like today's personal computer. Unfortunately, the concept was passed on for review by some senior executives who had recently been hired away from the Ford Motor Co. to improve the current "operations" of the enterprise. Their inward focus and their Ford-bred concern with "process" bridled their venturing spirit when it came to evaluating ambitious proposals for innovation and change. As a consequence, they failed to see an immediate competitive return on such investment, and dismissed a concept that could have eventually produced enormous, Microsoft-like successes in a burgeoning field of opportunity.

GET BASHED

While critics seem to abound in this day and age, it's still tough for a boss to get an accurate evaluation of his or her job performance.

Q. My business has grown rapidly in the past ten years and I've had to make the transition from entrepreneur to manager. Dealing with thirty employees is a different ballgame entirely. I've had no training for this. How can I tell if I'm doing it right?

A. Ask the critics who have the most to gain or lose because of your performance......your employees. Getting feedback from underlings is a delicate task, but it can be done in a way that benefits all parties.

Since most followers will be reluctant to proffer criticism of the boss, it takes special effort to flip the traditional top-down performance appraisal process so the "peons can pan their prince (or princess)."

Typically, "boss bashing" programs facilitating such upward evaluation involve structured questionnaires that are filled out, anonymously, by a manager's subordinates. These rating forms commonly evaluate the boss with respect to things like communication skills and policies; the allocation of unit or individual workloads; coaching and counseling practices; performance review and compensation skills; methods for achieving commitment and desired contributions from each team member; adroitness in handling crises; and the ability to find and solicit the best that an employee has to offer. Of course, there are many other criteria that you can apply in the formulation of your "report card."

Employees are well qualified to see—and criticize—their boss's routine activities since they have a ringside seat at the spectacle of him or her in action. Importantly, their unique perspective makes them experts when it comes to determining what is needed to motivate or move the "worker bees" in the organization.

An opportunity to participate in such an important process can also foster an atmosphere of openness that will encourage other forms of valuable employee expression.

Even a simple, homemade survey can be of immeasurable help in opening doors to communication, fostering an attitude of openness, and producing some worthwhile criticism for consideration by all involved. Any thick-skinned manager should be able to compile a list of performance characteristics for consideration by his subordinates. Once prepared, these criteria can be included in a simple form that allows a rater to quantitatively grade you with respect to each item.

Here are a few rules you should follow in implementing such an evaluation:

- Make sure that your employees understand the purpose of the evaluation, the technique used and its implications. They must fully appreciate the importance of thoughtful, truthful responses.

- Show them how this exercise will benefit both them and the company.

- Keep the population of raters large enough to be meaningful but small enough to be manageable. Five or six raters constitute the minimum survey population.

- Guarantee anonymity and confidentiality. A third-party administrator or facilitator can be employed to give your employees the assurance that the results of their efforts will be used only for the purposes declared. If they even suspect that retributional behavior could be the response to their efforts, their comments will be skewed to produce only favorable reactions and the entire undertaking will come to naught.

- Provide some type of "after action" report to your subordinates once the exercise has been completed. The report can range from a simple, grateful acknowledgment to a review of some of the findings with appropriate responses from you. Whatever tack is taken, it is important that something happens once the survey is completed. Your followers deserve recognition for their efforts. However, great pains should be taken to insure that they do not labor under the misapprehension that their responses, once tabulated and reviewed, will cause an immediate, earth-shaking change in your deportment. The goal of this kind of effort is to help you modify—where possible—and where not contrary to your fundamental beliefs or behavior patterns—your long-term approach to the tasks essential to the discharge of your responsibilities.

Indeed, you might not be the only party for which change is prescribed by the results of this upward evaluation. Frequently, a project like this provides a boss with information and insights that can help him assess ways in which he might endeavor to alter the attitudes and performance patterns of his subordinates.

While boss-bashing is, understandably, most warmly embraced by bosses who—in their minds, at least—are doing a good job and are loved by their employees, this type of analytical tool can be of tremendous benefit in high-stress circumstances where dissatisfaction and animosity are rife. In these kinds of situations, managers can easily lose touch with their charges and, as a consequence, become isolated to such a degree that they are prevented from effectively carrying out their responsibilities. Boss-bashing exercises can help a manager-under-siege open communications, modify his behavior, mend his fences and achieve self-salvation before it is too late.

In sum, your willingness to risk a bit of anarchy can reward you with a knowledge that enables you to polish your performance while pumping your team's productivity. Everybody benefits.

HOLD THE EDGE

It's what you learn after you know it all that counts.

—John Wooden, Coach

Lewis Carroll once defined education as "reeling, writhing and different branches of arithmetic—ambition, distraction, uglification and
derision." A career in business, however, demands a different kind of
learning.

Q. Some of my employees have their hearts set on becoming managers. I've told them they must first learn how to be entrepreneurs! What
type of education should they be seeking to best qualify for advancement?

A. Unlike the sciences and other structured professions such as law
and teaching, there's no proven educational path for those seeking
fame and fortune as venturers. Studies show that, while successful
entrepreneurs and business owners generally boast educational attain-
ments beyond those of the average person, they typically trail the educational accomplishments of professional managers. Quite a few of the
most successful "lead dogs" in venturing, like Bill Gates, dropped out
before completing college.

Some experts believe that entrepreneurial talent is gene-sourced, i.e.
you have to be born with it. However, a much larger body of evidence
supports management guru Peter Drucker's assertion that innovative
behavior can be learned...but not in the same way we mastered our
A,B,C's. Many colleges and universities have introduced one or more
"entrepreneurship" courses into their curricula, and a few have struc-

tured "majors" that focus primarily on developing entrepreneurial talent. Among the institutions that offer promising concentrations are Baylor, Babson, Wichita State, DePaul, and St. Thomas (Minneapolis). Karl Vesper at the University of Washington has compiled a compendium of the syllabi of many of the entrepreneurship courses taught throughout the United States.

The most valuable formal courses directly expose students to information, cases, and knowledge application opportunities that are grounded in reality. After all, when it comes to entrepreneurship, "experience is the best teacher."

Traditionally, a teacher gave the pupil who gazed out of the classroom window poorer grades than the one who buried his nose in a book. Today, we know that imagination is as important as memorization and that all the stuff we need to know won't be found in books. (As an entrepreneurship professor, I always encourage my graduating seniors to supplement their four years of scholarly pursuit with some "how to" adult education courses, a bit of Dale Carnegie-type help, and maybe some dancing and golf lessons…in order to get the tools necessary to profitably apply all of the nice knowledge they accumulated.)

Most entrepreneurs claim that it was what they saw, rather than what they studied, that gave them their key idea and the vision to successfully pursue it. They generally credit "previous experience" and a "keen eye" as the avenues to new venture discovery and the capacity to convert opportunity to profit.

Entrepreneurship is an art, not a science. The Greeks recognized that there were techniques ("techne") that could not be explained in words but learned only through apprenticeship and experience. Therefore, the educational programs that are most successful are the ones that convert ad hoc experience into information, analogies, anecdotes and case studies that can be systematically conveyed. The best "courses" are typically the ones taught by educationists who have had personal experience as venturers. Practice is more important than theory in this field of endeavor, so a pedigreed professor with little real-world exposure is a lot like a pediatrician who never had kids.

This is not to say that your employees should forsake formal education. Experience without the means to understand it can produce as much frustration as a trip without a destination.

Brass Tacks Tip: Advise your employees to learn from everything they do whether it be listening to a lecture or watching 'toons on TV. Their future success—and yours—will depend on a perpetually maintained ability to combine formal learning and personal experience into a unique blend of actionable knowledge.

It's important to note that, in today's fast changing world, none of us can ever risk believing that our education is complete. Indeed, we are all "temporary help," and we will retain our employability only if we continue to stay relevant through continuing education.

These days, the typical job has a much shorter life span than the person who occupies it. If a person falls off the "work wagon" without adequate education and experience, he or she will, most assuredly, become "obsolete" with a very limited future. Contemporary companies flourish only with informed, aware and educated leaders at the helm. Not too long ago, the only things that became rapidly obsolete were women's hats, automobiles like the Edsel, and W.C. Field's membership in Alcoholics Anonymous. These days it's a different story. A business owner or manager can be "hot" one day and "not" the next.

In the good old days, we were able to easily track the age and obsolescence of automobiles. "There goes a '49 Ford!" "Hey, how about that '55 Impala?" "Man, didja see that '47 Hudson Hornet?" It won't be long before we'll be identifying recently obsoleted workers by the year their trek to obsolescence actually commenced—the year of their college commencement. "Look at that poor '82 Harvard!" "Do you believe the wear on that '79 UCLA?" "We couldn't even place that '90 Notre Dame in the swap sheets!!" Indeed, we'll probably classify aging matriculated students by their outmoded "accessories." Instead of lamenting their out-of-date fender fins or Dyna-Flow, we'll be heaping scorn on their MBAs or PhDs.

It's tough to admit that the knowledge and abilities that we accumulate during the years of our formal education endure far less well than the yellowed lecture notes of the faculty members who regaled us in class. Fact is, the "half-life" of a college education is now only slightly more than four years.

The theories, postulates and facts of yesterday are ever more quickly becoming the oddities of today. Their usefulness in helping a person hang on to a worthwhile position in business is eroding more rapidly than ever before in history. Today, a shift from relevance to residue can occur in a nanosecond.

That's why picking the right education, training and experience is one of the most important undertakings of every person with aspirations and ambition. The second most important endeavor in any career is to keep that knowledge fresh.

The need for continuing education is more obvious than ever. Whether we bounce back to our alma maters, crawl the Internet, or sign on for courses from a trade or professional association, we must, of necessity, work unceasingly to keep ourselves current and relevant. In this era of lightning change, sheepskins can get sheared all too rapidly.

Indeed, I've often believed that colleges and universities should offer a "warranty" with the degrees they hand out on commencement day. After all, it works for Ford, Chrysler and GM. Our academic "body shops" should offer whatever continuing education programs are necessary to keep an alum's BS or BA in cruising condition. They don't have to do it for free; but they should do it willingly and well.

This means the tenured gentry on today's campuses are going to have to keep learning new tricks and new methods for teaching them. Corporations will have to open their facilities more generously to faculty members who want to learn "what's happening" at the very points at which it is happening. Publishers will have to switch from printed tomes that are out of date by the time they hit bookstore shelves, to new teaching mechanisms like computerized simulations, interactive learning systems, web-based training, and experience-sharing video conferencing with the people who've "been there; done that."

With your knowledge and abilities—and those of your work-force—being obsoleted as rapidly as they are, it is up to you to continually provide your employees with access to appropriate continuing educational programs and real-time opportunities to broaden their experience.

NURTURE THE KNOW HOW

He who resolves never to ransack any mind but his own will soon be reduced, from mere barrenness, to the poorest of all imitations: he will be obliged to imitate himself.

—Sir Joshua Reynolds, Patron of the arts

Aggressive entrepreneurs and managers are always looking for an edge—a critical difference in modus operandi that will give them a distinct advantage in the marketplace.

Q. I think I've read every "how-to book" for managers and, as a consequence, I have accumulated more information about the "keys to success" than I'll ever be able to use. But I still haven't found the "basic ingredient" needed to stay a step ahead of the competition. Can you sum up your best advice in one sentence?

A. I'll do better than that. One word says it all: KNOWLEDGE. The true EDGE in business is derived from the unique knowledge that a firm's employees—all of them, individually and collectively—possess, create and share. Indeed, the last four letters of the word "knowledge" describe what prize can be won if this precious resource is harvested and used properly.

The process of innovation—the key to successful entrepreneurial behavior—involves discovery (looking outward for information and insights), creativity (searching within yourself for new ideas) and knowledge building and sharing (taking all the information gleaned in the first two steps and putting it to work). Knowledge is a fuel mined by heads, not hands, and is the primary propellant of continuous innovation.

Brass Tacks Tip: A company's edge in its markets is principally a function of the quantity, quality and use of the knowledge at its command. Management guru Peter Drucker has asserted that knowledge is not just one resource among the traditional, principal factors of production—labor, capital, and land—but it is the *only meaningful* resource.

In their book, <u>The Knowledge Creating Company</u>, Professors Ikujiro Nonaka and Hirotaka Takeuchi draw a distinction between tacit knowledge and explicit knowledge.

"Explicit knowledge," they say, is "codified" knowledge that can be communicated in formal, systematic language. It is easily traded and shared. This is the stuff that computers love to process, teachers love to teach, and number crunchers love to crunch. We can send it over the Internet or store it in our databases. It comes in many forms and is available from many sources. Any aggressive enterprise can access it.

"Tacit knowledge," on the other hand, is highly personal and hard to convey in formalized language. One form of tacit knowledge is experience-bred know-how of the type that distinguishes master craftsmen like heart surgeons, musicians, golf champions and diamond cutters. It's almost impossible to explain or impart via typical teaching methodologies. It's usually conveyed through apprenticeships where students can "absorb" the knowledge as it is being applied and expanded, thus developing ownership through use. (A sub-category is "cognitive tacit knowledge," which consists of extremely personal mental models, beliefs and perceptions that individuals build within themselves over time.) Such knowledge is a person's unique possession and reflects his or her image of reality. It consists of insights, intuition and hunches as well as concepts acquired along life's path.

Since tacit knowledge is very subjective and comes inconveniently packaged in human psyches, it's not easy to access, convey or share. Nevertheless, a firm's true edge is derived from its ability to convert this elusive commodity into explicit, manageable knowledge for its own exclusive use.

Tacit knowledge has to be gingerly extracted by the leaders of an enterprise and given "handles" to make it portable and useable by others within the firm, both individually and collectively. This is how priceless new knowledge, essential to a firm's innovative strength, is created and made available for use.

By continuously stimulating interaction among employees and guiding those exchanges carefully, managers can filter and cross-pollinate knowledge within a firm's own walls. As a consequence, new knowledge will be perpetually manufactured, creating an institutional asset that is truly powerful. Indeed, no other firm can posses this same advantage. A company's body of proprietary knowledge is as unique as the fingerprints of its employees and more valuable than any other asset on its balance sheet. It is this asset that can provide the company with an unbeatable edge.

Given the potential of this awesome resource, enlightened managers must know how to hire and stimulate employees who are capable of readily consuming information, experience, ideas and insights, and producing new personal knowledge that can be shared and applied. A firm's leaders are obliged to make sure that all employees understand their responsibility to continuously hunt, dress and digest new intellectual prey. Owners and their managers must also develop the interpersonal skills necessary to systematically elicit this know-how from their team members, format it, make it communicable and understandable, and distribute it to those areas of the enterprise where it will do the most good.

In the words of Dostoevsky, "There is no subject so old that something new cannot be said about it."

SHARE THE WEALTH

All for one, one for all.

—Alexandre Dumas, Novelist and playwright

A firm's most valuable asset is the individual and collective knowledge of its employees, a resource that can provide an enterprise with an unparalleled edge in the marketplace. But a business owner must know how to tap into this valuable commodity.

Q. You've made a strong case for building and sharing knowledge in an enterprise. Any recommendations for getting employees to open up and exchange what they have with others?

A. Gold has no value until it is mined. The same holds true for ideas and insights. The trick is to create an environment that encourages individual self-expression, even if an employee isn't completely confident that his or her contribution has value. Most people must feel "safe" in order to expose themselves in untested or unproven ways. It's your job, therefore, to provide a non-threatening forum for expression. Despite the fact that today's workforce is the most highly educated in history, many employees still shrink from risking embarrassment or becoming the butt of an unfavorable critique.

Hence, they are reluctant to associate themselves (and their hoped for careers) with a wild or crazy—or simply dumb—idea. 'Tis better, they believe, to be frustrated than to be ridiculed. As a consequence, the bulk of this nation's creative, innovative, intellectual and experience-bred power goes unused.

Here are a few Brass Tacks Tips for boosting the flow and exchange of knowledge in your firm:

- <u>Make sure your employees share a broad, inclusive vision of your company's potential</u>. The bigger the canvas, the more expressive the picture they can create. A specific, unilateral mission statement that comes down from "the top" will narrow the receivers' thinking and discourages "non-conforming," creative contributions.

- <u>Maintain an atmosphere of "uncertainty," not certainty</u>. If workers feel that you know everything—and that they should—they will be reluctant to show themselves as foragers, finders, and explorers, which are essential roles of a thinker. Its been said that "lack of discovery is the price we pay for certainty."

- <u>Use meetings, not memos</u>. People in group gatherings tend to cross-pollinate, to share ideas and build on them as open discourse progresses. Problem solving and brainstorming both work better where open communication and free participation are encouraged.

- <u>Work in teams, not committees</u>. The purpose of a committee is to reach acceptable consensus on an issue. This is usually achieved by forcing compromise through the "dumbing" down of each individual's contribution. The goal of a team, however, is operational. A team is tasked to meet a challenge, solve a problem, or effect a tangible result. Its success is not predicated on watered-down agreement but on decisive action that is based on the very best input available.

- <u>Trade, don't teach</u>. Information is conveyed most effectively through free exchange, not through a lecture.

- <u>Use metaphors, not manuals</u>. Truly unique ideas and experiences are generally difficult to express cogently in words. Diamond cutters, blacksmiths and artists are typically hard-pressed to "explain" what they do. The use of examples or related situations to infer, illustrate or indirectly describe are frequently helpful. Similes using the words "like" or "as" can relate unlike things comparatively to make something clear.

- Use intimacy, eschew formality. The manager and the managed should share personal knowledge of one another. A "comfortable" friendship, wherein personal familiarity is encouraged, will breed more open, unintimidated, well-purposed exchanges of beliefs, opinions and experience.

- Rely on tolerance, not templates. Be willing to allow people to do things their way, to experiment, and—perish the thought—fail without fear of unreasonable retribution. It's the only way you'll get people to really open up and generate knowledge that is new, different, and unique. Rigid guidelines, precise measurement standards, and templates for "acceptable" performance are not acceptable in the achievement-oriented firm.

- Interrogate; don't be indifferent. Often, the only way to learn something is to ask. And once somebody opens up, don't forget the three most important words in an inquisitive boss's vocabulary: "Tell me more."

- Supply active approbation, not passive acceptance. Be generous and sincere in expressing your appreciation for the knowledge your employees contribute. Sure, they get paid for doing their job, but remember, you want much more than that. You should demand the best your employees can give, and the rewards they receive should reflect the value they proffer.

GIVE 'EM THE TOOLS THEY NEED

Give me where to stand, and I will move the earth.

—Archimedes, Mathematician

Creative, innovative, industrious managers are a hot commodity these days. The owners of companies know that the quality of their leaders determines the success of their ventures.

Proven managers appreciate this fact, too, and, as a consequence, many are putting a higher price on the unique contributions they can make.

Q. I own a fairly large business and keeping my managers motivated is a top priority. I pay salaries that are very competitive, but it doesn't seem to be doing the trick. Any Brass Tacks Tips?

A. Importantly, cash compensation and monetary benefits are not your employees' only motivations. Managers know that in order to be successful—and to achieve personal fulfillment—they must share in the kinds of policy formulation and decision-making that traditionally were the exclusive province of the owners of the enterprise.

As a result, managers worth their salt are demanding a place at the owner's table from the time policy is made to the point that the rewards are divvied up. Their demands are being met, too. The prevailing tight labor market for superior managers has given present-day talent-sellers a distinct advantage.

But even if this were not the case, business owners should be delighted to share their power and position with managers. In today's change-a-minute world, opportunities come and go at warp speed, make-or-break challenges are ever-present, and competition is relentless. Therefore, companies need the best and brightest talent available. To attract it and retain it they must be willing to maintain a challenging and rewarding work environment that provides managers with the participation, perks and passion of ownership.

In a start-up entrepreneurial venture, one just has to hang up a shingle to acquire ownership status. But in a large, established company, the acquisition of "ownership" by salaried managers is a bit more difficult.

VIRTUAL OWNERSHIP: THE ULTIMATE ENERGIZER, a program offered by the Center for Business Ownership Inc., shows both the "givers" and "receivers" of ownership entitlements just what is required in order to reap the benefits of shared ownership.

The Center contends that an enterprise must provide its managers—its virtual owners—with:

- Access to all of the financial and operating information they need for effective policy formulation and decision-making. Today, a manager's "need to know" cannot be tightly circumscribed. It's impossible to foretell which piece of data might inspire a new, innovative initiative with respect to product development, process improvement, pricing, marketing and the like.

- A worthwhile mission that challenges managers abilities. This mandate must make sense to both the firm and the managers who are expected to implement it.

- An opportunity to participate in the formulation of the strategies and goals that define that mission. Managers must become "owners" of the goal they are pursuing. If they "are there at the creation," and if the objectives they formulate reflect their personal insights and ambitions, they will be self-driven to deliver the desired outcomes.

- License to continually and aggressively seek and exploit new revenue streams to fuel the firm in the future. The lifecycles of most market offerings are continually growing shorter. Since tomorrow's products are today's visions, managers must be encouraged to forge and pursue those visions.

- The resources—especially knowledge and technology—that are necessary to do the job. Management guru Peter Drucker claims that knowledge will be the most important corporate resource in the twenty-first century. Managers must have the tools with which to create; the technology with which they can compete.

- The freedom to be innovative, assume risk and take the initiative. Managers must have the authority, time and liberty to experiment and break the rules. They must be empowered to "creatively destroy" old ways of doing things and "constructively innovate" the new.

- The right to eschew traditional lockstep planning in favor of "Pathfinding™"—serendipitous opportunity exploitation—in the pursuit of tactical, short-term objectives. For a motivated, able, ambitious and nimble manager, goals and guidelines are all that is needed.

- The right to grant opportunity and independence to energetic, innovative—sometimes eccentric—followers through "mission contracts" that convey broad delegation of authority and responsibility. Managers must be allowed to truly empower their disciples to do what they want to do, not what the person who conveys the power wants them to do.

- Permission to mobilize into team-units—or other types of organizational components—that are part of a fluid, flexible structure that facilitates communication, decision-making, proactive implementation and rapid response to opportunity.

- Economic rewards commensurate with achievement. A "piece of the action" is essential for an individual who is expected to perform entrepreneurially. While the monetary payoffs of "ownership" can take many forms, they must transcend those afforded by traditional salary and benefit packages. They can take the form of actual equity entitlements like stock awards, stock options or ESOPs, or Virtual Equity™ participation such as "phantom" stock, shared appreciation rights or profit sharing.

This is a tall, but essential, order. In the future, the success of an enterprise will be a direct result of the entrepreneurial talents of managers *who feel like they own the joint.*

CELEBRATE INDEPENDENCE

All good work is done in defiance of management.
—Bob Woodward, Pulitzer Prize winning journalist

We have often emphasized the importance of giving an employee a "free hand" with respect to the execution of delegated responsibility.

Q. Just how far can you go in delegating authority to employees? After all, as the owner of the business, I am ultimately responsible for what everybody does.

A. Fact is, if you want someone to help you make your business all it can be, he or she is going to have to be free to apply their talents as only they can. Said another way, if you want your followers to act entrepreneurially, you'll have to afford them the kind of freedom, independence and self-determination that motivates entrepreneurs to achieve.

Keep in mind, the reason that entrepreneurial personalities most frequently give for starting their own businesses is "to achieve independence." Similarly, almost two-thirds of entrepreneurs say they started their venture to "be their own boss." One-third did it in order to have control over their personal fortunes. Only three percent did it for the money!

These data strongly suggest that a progressive business owner has to accept a clear "declaration of independence" from the people to whom he or she has delegated responsibility for superior accomplishment. Your followers must have a big arena—free from conventions and constraints—in which to create. They must feel free to explore and experiment as they execute. It's the only way you can expect truly EUREKA-type innovations.

It's your job to protect your followers from the blight of organizational bureaucracy. This is particularly important if the people to whom you are delegating responsibility are managers themselves. You are counting on them to experiment, diverge, take risks and seek the "new and different" in the pursuit of constructive innovation. You want lions, not sheep, so keep in mind the words of a former president of 3M Corp.: "If you put fences around people, you get sheep."

Brass Tacks Tip: A creative worker is typically inclined to act like the proverbial "house eccentric," so you must be prepared to give him or her dispensation from your otherwise rational "house rules." The achievements of innovative people are a function of what you let them achieve. Often, this means permitting them to depart from reasonable standards of organizational conduct. (Check out <u>Re-Inventing the Future</u> by Thomas Bass. He closely examined the lives of eleven prominent scientists and concludes that creativity is, indeed, very closely linked to independence.)

If you are a "classic" entrepreneur, you are, by nature, a control freak who strives to control your time, environment, timetables and the events that can affect your accomplishment. By contrast, a truly innovative employee will typically want to do things his way, on his timetable. So, to achieve your goals, you'll probably have to give your followers flexibility with respect to things like scheduling, resource utilization and the like. At 3M Corp., for example, research technicians have been allowed up to 15% of their time to work on a project of their choosing, regardless of corporate priorities. An entrepreneurial personality needs time to explore—to "diddle and dawdle" in the pursuit of exploitable opportunities.

The unique, sometimes permissive, accommodations you afford them might extend to dress, hours of work, their personal "space," compensation and job title. In the days when computers were first being adopted by business enterprises, the main frames and the "different" folk who knew how to fire them up were often housed in facilities apart from the digs housing "normal" business functions. This was because good computer geeks were hard to come by, so they had to be granted exceptions from normal corporate standards of dress and deportment. Furthermore, as a scarce resource that was in great demand, their compensation was outside the normal company "scale." Therefore, it was hoped that by housing them off campus, they would not taint the behavior or expectations of the "mainstream" employees.

Today, many of the exceptional "latitudes" that these kinds of workers once clandestinely enjoyed are routinely shared by everyone in an enterprise. The value of far-sighted, creative—albeit eccentric—innovators is being recognized far and wide. In recent years, places like Silicon Valley have embraced the "bring your dog to work" approach in attracting and retaining high-powered talent.

Indeed, companies in a wide range of industries are now investing considerable sums in "skunkworks," organizational components that are specially designed to stimulate and accommodate entrepreneurial talent. These facilities are, in effect, "hothouses" for growing ideas.

Remember, the typical entrepreneur has a great deal of trouble with authority figures. This means that in an ideal situation he or she will make you, the owner/boss, feel challenged, criticized, and bereft of control. Tom Peters says that, "If a follower doesn't treat you like a jerk, and doesn't think differently than you, one of you is redundant." He goes on to say, "Anybody who agrees with you should be fired."

George Bernard Shaw observed that "all progress depends on the unreasonable man." He believed that a "reasonable" man would adapt himself to the world, accepting that which is. Thus, he'll never discover anything better. The unreasonable man, he concluded, will never stop trying to adapt the world to himself and his ideas. It is the unreasonable man, therefore, who will be responsible for the change that is essential to progress.

KEEP IT SIMPLE

It is very hard to be simple enough to be good.

—Ralph Waldo Emerson, Writer

For the foreseeable future, most companies will rely on some kind of formal organizational structure. But, given the pace of change nowadays, most will have to alter their structures significantly and frequently, moving away from the pyramidal, hierarchical, layered, top-down forms that have prevailed for most of economic history.

Q. In a previous column you espoused doing away with most formal corporate organizational structures. This would never fly in my company. Any suggestions short of abolition??

A. Understandably, it will be a while before most businesses embrace with gleeful abandon an anarchical approach to organizational design. Nevertheless, they will have to strive mightily to make sure their organizational structures, whatever their formal design, are simple, flexible, flat, participative and decentralized.

In the future, organizations of every size will have to work to "keep it simple" so that its key employees can easily understand how the entire enterprise works as a whole and how its functions are related. As a result, each will be able to occupy an optimally productive spot in the scheme of things, making highest and best use of their individual talents (as well as the technology that is made available to them). An appropriately simple structure will afford its inhabitants a quick, firm grasp on prevailing reality and the flexibility to make frequent and meaningful tactical adjustments.

- <u>Flexibility is essential</u>. Organizations must be malleable and nimble enough to quickly facilitate—and readily dismantle—new component units, joint ventures, alliances, coalitions and partnerships on an ad hoc basis to take maximum advantage of a market opportunity. A capacity for quick adaptation and exploitation is a must, and this requires a simple organizational design.

- <u>Decentralization is a must</u>. Small, independent operating units are more able to appropriately design and rapidly implement the tasks that quickly become essential in a fast moving environment. (Centralization engenders an inward/upward focus that tends to be conditioned by what prevailed in the organization's past and what the leaders' perceptions "might be" rather than by what is screaming for attention in the present.)

- <u>"Flatness" is crucial</u>. An enterprise's adaptability is inversely related to the number of structural layers it embraces. The "flatter" an entity, the faster it can function. Fewer layers of intermediate management improve communication, innovation and execution since all "worker bees" are closer to the "queen," and her (or his) hive is closer to the marketplace <u>and</u> its demands. Change can be understood and implemented rapidly if communication and counsel do not have to wend their way, tortuously, through level upon level of people who feel compelled to contribute their two cents. It has been said that a blueberry pancake embodies the organizational characteristics required in the modern corporations. It's flat, thin and the berries—its distinguishing and critical components—are distributed as the physics of the prevailing situation demand.

Keep in mind that the elimination of layers of managers and supervisors levies a tremendous leadership burden on those who remain in the few remaining strata. In the days of "deep' organizations with many plateaus of managers, each work director would typically supervise six or seven followers. Today, given the reduction in organizational tiers, a leader has to manage many more followers in order to maintain an equivalent of customer-contact personnel at the fringe of the enterprise. The span currently runs from fifteen to twenty persons, but experts tell us that, in order to maintain this kind of efficiency in tomorrow's world, a leader will have direct responsibility for as many as twenty-five to thirty followers.

In the near-term future, most truly successful business organizations will reflect one or more of the following key structural characteristics:

- <u>Self-organization</u>: Ad hoc, project-tasked groups of individuals with a common mission will be created (or will self-organize) with increased frequency in order to achieve what is immediately required by the firm's strategic and tactical goals. The constituents of <u>these</u> teams will be essentially self-directed, and their members will collaboratively allocate responsibilities among themselves according to the highest and best use of their individual talents. Such teams will demonstrate a very personal collaboration in which a leader leads by participating. In addition to being a "pathfinder" and monitoring progress, a leader will also link teams and their output to other teams in the network and, ultimately, to the end achievements that have been targeted by the enterprise.

- <u>Intrapreneurial</u>: A growing number of organizational units will be dedicated exclusively to creating unique value through entrepreneurial innovation and industriousness. The term "intrapreneurship" was coined several years ago to characterize these kinds of efforts. In essence, they will constitute independent businesses within an existing firm. Companies like 3-M, Johnson & Johnson and Motorola have actually recruited entrepreneurial personalities to form new enterprises within their "womb" that can be eventually spun off as full-fledged, profit-making businesses. Such structural demarcation allows for the kind of independence, motivation and compensation that entrepreneurial leaders need to create new and different products or services that will ensure the firm's future.

- <u>Nuclear</u>: More and more large and structurally complex companies will also function as incubators, spinning-off significant, stand-alone components of their evolving operations into independent companies, divisions or subsidiaries. Once again, this kind of de-structuring provides for more aggressive, inspired entrepreneurial exploitation.

- <u>Virtual</u>: Some companies will exist only as collaborations with other existing (perhaps even competing) business entities. Such "partnering" through strategic alliances and joint ventures will permit rapid and powerful responses to opportunities. Each <u>participating</u> entity will contribute only those talents or resources that the at-hand task requires—and only for so long as the task requires them. Such connections will be easily and inexpensively created, disassembled and, if warranted, rejoined—perhaps with different participants—to take advantage of new and different opportunities in the marketplace as quickly as they emerge.

With new forms of organization like this, you will become what UCLA Professor Karen Stephenson calls a "hub," "gatekeeper" or "pulse-taker." In addition to being an innovative, change-making entrepreneurial force, you'll have to serve as: a "hub" who knows the shortest path to everyone and every necessary achievement in the organization; a "gatekeeper" who facilitates an informational bridge between different groups; and a pulse-taker" who knows what everyone else is thinking and feeling. Your fundamental task will, of course, be to monitor ongoing accomplishment, ensuring that it accommodates the instant mission of the enterprise.

In the words of statesman Henry Kissinger, such challenging new organizational forms will be absolutely essential to "......get your people from where they are to where they have not been."

SEARCH FOR THE BEST

All successful employers are stalking men who will do the unusual, men who think, men who attract attention by performing more than is expected of them.

—Charles M. Schwab, Entrepreneur

For the first time since World War II, the number one gripe of small business operators—high taxes—has dropped to second place on their list of laments. Their biggest problem nowadays is finding capable workers.

Q. My small business is doing very well, but I'm missing out on incredible growth opportunities because I'm not able fill the jobs with the kind of employees that will enable me to muster the "followership" I need. Any suggestions for improving my recruiting record?

A. Don't despair. You're not alone. Almost 75% of today's small business owners claim they are having a difficult time finding qualified workers. Your challenge is to establish a modus operandi for recruiting that is superior to that of everyone else on the talent search circuit. Since people are your most important resource, you have to make "talent trapping" your number one priority—along with the umpteen other tasks that vie for top position on your CEO To Do List.

A small business needs innovative, industrious, self-starters who easily see the "big picture" and move quickly to assume responsibility for its achievement. These are the same characteristics that are sought by the promoters of start-up ventures and the HR types at large, benefit-rich corporations, so you have to position and pitch your firm—and the opportunities it offers—in a manner that makes a job at your shop more appealing than any alternative.

Here are a few ***Brass Tacks Tips*** that should help you do that.

- <u>Don't overlook any opportunity to prospect</u>. Network with friends, family and fellow alumni. Boast unashamedly, in any forum you can find, about the incredible opportunity your firm offers a worker with above-average aspirations. Good "buzz" about your company will attract resumes. Supplement the flow with tantalizing ads in media that are not commonly used for the purpose of recruiting. Alternative newspapers, theater programs, church bulletins and targeted radio spots can give you a unique edge.

- <u>Read every resume you get</u>. Search to find a partial fit, at least. Good orientation and training can fill in many up-front gaps in an applicant's expertise or experience.

- <u>Be willing to personally interview a prospect at any time, at any place</u>. Be ready to convey a compelling vision of your firm's future in a way that demonstrates a unique personal opportunity for the candidate. Today's capable workers don't want to underutilize their precious time and talent, and they want to know that you appreciate that fact. Don't be surprised if you are asked for a copy of your business plan.

- <u>Rent-to- buy</u>. Use temporary help with the intention of signing on good talent when you find it. You'll probably have to pay extra for such a right of conversion, but the help in recruiting and the "free look" you'll receive will probably be worth it.

- <u>Establish internships for young people still in school</u>. This kind of opportunity to learn and earn creates good first impressions that can often be expanded into enduring connections. Most colleges have coordinators who can help you.

- <u>Use your web site to troll for talent</u>. But make sure the site is easily navigable and user friendly. Succinctly explain your firm's open positions and the benefits it offers. Allow visitors to explore and respond with a minimum of clicks. Require just enough feedback for you to follow-up.

- <u>Till where others fail to tread</u>. Over 80% of today's retirees say they want to work past age sixty-five. Give 'em a chance. Start networking with them before they pull the plug on their careers. Many of them are delaying opportunities to retire from dead-end jobs because they're afraid they'll have no place to go. Canvass senior citizen centers and golf courses for those who have already had their ticket punched but are eager to stay relevant. Sam Walton taught us all a lesson in this regard. Also, connect with cultural and ethnic groups to recruit recent émigrés and refugees. These folks typically have a tremendous drive to succeed and prove themselves and, of course, gain permanent residency. Be prepared to offer language courses and to change the lunchroom menu—small prices to pay for good talent. Also, connect with groups that aid the handicapped. Many jobs can be modified to accommodate these eager and uniquely able workers who are too often overlooked. Finally, don't rule out rehab centers, government sponsored work-to-welfare programs and halfway houses. They often harbor appetent souls who are willing to work hard for a fresh start.

- <u>Offer relevant returns</u>. Most large firms can't offer the time accommodations (e.g. flextime, part-time, special vacation scheduling, etc.) and place-pliancy (e.g. telecommuting, home-based assignments, etc.) that you probably can. Consider restructuring full-time positions into part-time opportunities with pay and benefits that more closely mirror those enjoyed by full-time workers. Don't be afraid to ask prospects what special accommodations would favorably dispose them to your firm. The cost of these adjustments could be relatively minor given the revenues you are now missing because of your inability to field an adequate workforce.

- <u>Consider signing bonuses for attractive candidates</u>. Also, "bounties" can be offered to current employees for their scouting services that result in new hires.

- <u>Offer more than a salary</u>. Ambitious workers also want a chance to get special training and experience. You have to be ready to help <u>people</u> enhance their personal worth so that they can tap even more valuable opportunities in the future. Remember, too, that today's workers are entrepreneurially oriented and covet a "piece of the action." Their "Bill Gates envy" can often be assuaged with perfor-mance-based "virtual equity" like profit sharing programs, shared appreciation rights, phantom stock and actual stock ownership with properly structured "puts" and "calls" that take into account the needs of all parties.

Keep in mind, "these times they are-a-changin'." Understand what new additions of talent will accrue the greatest benefit to your firm and be prepared to do what you must to recruit them to your service. Today's employer has to be a lot more flexible than the HR director of yore. When the Pony Express needed riders in the late 1800's, it simply ran this ad: "Wanted: Young, skinny, wiry fellows, not over 18. Orphans preferred." These days you've got to offer a lot more than "happy trails."

PROVIDE A PIECE OF THE ACTION

Life is a misery if you don't get more than you deserve.

—Harry Oppenheimer, Executive

"Where your treasure is, there will your heart be also." (Matthew 6:21) Today, in the business world, we simplify by saying: "Where the pocketbook beckons, the spirit will follow."

Q. In your columns, you've emphasized the importance of employees feeling like "owners" as a consequence of the nature of their work. Are you saying that only a small part of the ownership equation involves the ownership of stock??

A. Absolutely not. We emphasized the non-monetary aspects of "ownership" simply because so little attention is commonly paid to the important psychic feeling of ownership. But the pecuniary "piece of the action" is equally important.

Entrepreneurs enjoy equity from day one. Traditionally, employees never got an opportunity to participate in stock ownership of the firm. These days superior performance is essential to the success of any enterprise; and to get this type of talent, firms are having to pay more than a nice salary and some "plain vanilla" benefits. Top employees want in-the-pocket rewards like those afforded the proprietors of the venture. And they are getting what they seek.

It's currently estimated that somewhere between forty-five and fifty percent of all employees enjoy stock options, a good surrogate indicator for actual stock ownership. This percentage is up from only twenty-five percent just five years ago. Furthermore, the percentage is actually higher for companies not classified as "small businesses." Over ninety percent of the Fortune 1000 firms use stock options, according to a survey by TPF&C, a Towers Perrin Company. Another survey by Ernst & Young shows that about forty-two percent of "fast-growth entrepreneurs" share ownership with employees as well as managers.

The National Center for Employee Ownership reports that about sixteen million employees benefit from stock ownership through stock bonus plans, 401K plans, broad stock option plans and formal Employee Stock Ownership Plans.

The reasons for the explosive growth in ownership entitlements are pretty clear.

First, employees want it. While wages and benefits offer security (the old "social contract" between employers and employees), actual stock ownership promises opportunity. Managers and key employees seek wages as payment for work that's been done; ownership entitlements are payment for what they'll do. Equity sharing programs give the talent-providers an opportunity to share the paybacks traditionally reserved for talent-users.

These days workers are spending a great deal of time, money and energy honing their skills. Many of them have particularly valuable abilities as knowledge workers, technicians or "people handlers." For critical talents, it is a sellers market; and the sellers are looking to share in the spoils of the success they produce.

Secondly, employers are beginning to appreciate what "more than money" can buy. Studies by the NCEO reveal that companies with employee owners grow eight to eleven percent a year faster than they would have if no ownership was granted. Other studies suggest that stock price performance of public companies with employee ownership is significantly better than that of firms with no such involvement. Indeed, a study by the University of Baltimore shows that fewer than one out of one hundred ESOPs were terminated because of the bankruptcy of the plan sponsor. An Employee Ownership Index created by American Capital Strategies, an investment-banking firm in Bethesda,

Maryland, reflects the "superior performance" of 350 public companies with at least ten-percent broad-based employee ownership. During the nineteen-nineties, EOI stock price performance was more than double that of both the Dow Jones Industrial Average and the S&P 500.

Perhaps this is why a recent poll revealed that seventy-three percent of employers favored sharing equity with employees. It's pretty clear that sharing ownership makes good bottom line sense.

Picking up on the positives of equity-sharing, Dana Rohrabacher, Republican Congressman form California, suggested that making mailmen shareholders might well be the answer to saving "the nation's most threatened corporation of all," the U.S. Post Office. He sponsored legislation that was designed to "give" the Postal Service to its 750,000 employees.

Shared ownership will be a pretty hard trend to buck as more employees begin to seek the increasing good fortune of their share-owning bosses. To see Jack Welch, the Chairman of the General Electric Company, blessed with $350 million of stock appreciation rights, restricted stock units, deferred compensation and stock options is one thing. To see the computer nerd across the street buy a new million-dollar mansion is something else. And it's happening. Allan Sloan, the Wall Street editor of <u>Newsweek</u>, calculated that on Thanksgiving 1997, the average paper profits per employee on Microsoft stock amounted to $1,000,000. This is a significant number considering that slightly less than ninety percent of Microsoft's employees enjoy stock options.

It's easy to see why a Gallup Organization survey reported that while twenty-three percent of surveyed employees would like to receive more cash in their paychecks right now, twenty-nine percent said they would rather have a share in the ownership of the company that could be cashed out when they leave the job.

While the psychic benefit associated with a role that affords employees a type of ownership participation in operating the business is an essential driver of performance, the old-fashioned appeal of equity-derived dollars is a powerful motivator also.

FOCUS ON THE TOP LINE

Everyone lives by selling something.

—Robert Louis Stevenson, Author

A successful entrepreneur quickly learns how to make the "highest and best use" of his or her unique venturing talents. The fortunes of a firm are determined by the entrepreneur's ability to focus this proprietary energy in the areas of activity that will produce the greatest results.

Q. All business people are taught to revere the "bottom line." This advice has prompted me to spend most of my time on managing costs, processes and systems to make sure I'm generating a profit. I've gotten good at it, but I don't feel that my company has taken off like it should have. Am I missing something?

A. Yes. You've overlooked the critical importance of your "top line." It is your firm's revenue stream—the sales that show up on the top line—which constitutes the fuel needed to propel your enterprise. Without an adequate flow of income, you'll never be able to get enough black ink to the bottom line to be satisfactorily profitable.

The "magic" that an entrepreneur brings to an enterprise occurs at the top of the income statement. It is because of his or her vision, optimism, product or service knowledge and boundless energy that stuff gets sold in the first place. It is his unparalleled optimism, ingenuity and persistence that keep the product moving.

It's this bundle of rare entrepreneurial traits that generates an adequate and consistent revenue stream, the lifeblood of any business. And it's his or her matchless marketing drive and customer contact skills that keep the stream flowing.

Most of the people who work for you probably don't have these magic-making abilities to the extent you manifest them. Therefore, your focus should be on the top line, while the more narrow and specialized talents of your employees are probably best used in the conversion of your marketplace magic into a bottom line. The managerial—as contrasted to entrepreneurial—skills they learned in business school will achieve the greatest payoff when concentrated on activities like procurement, production, expense control and systems development.

Of course, as the firm's leader-in-residence, you can't abandon these vital administrative processes, but the bulk of your time and creative juices should be devoted to those revenue-generating product, market and customer functions at which you excel. Management skills are critical, but they are readily available in today's workplace. A person like you, however, is hard to find. Not many people are capable of turning a vision into an opportunity and converting an opportunity into a business.

Brass Tacks Tip: "If ya got it, flaunt it." Don't fuss over the administrative details of your business. You can hire a capable person to do that for you. Keep your precious entrepreneurial eye on the top line from whence all good things will eventually come.

CONCENTRATE ON CONNECTIONS

To please people is a great step towards persuading them.
— Philip Dormer Stanhope, Statesman

In today's competitive, complex world, good marketing entails more than just making a profitable sale.

Q. I own a business that sells big-ticket items to other businesses. Any ideas as to how I can distinguish myself from the rest of the pack?

A. The key to what you seek lies in "relationship marketing," a technique that will help you attract and keep sophisticated, demanding customers in competitive business-to-business marketplaces.

Since all business success begins with the "top line" on the income statement, it's important to build strong, enduring sales connections with the owners and principals in the firms that constitute your primary market. Since you are probably going toe-to-toe with some big competitors, you'll be greatly advantaged if you individualize and personalize your approaches to these decision-makers.

As you know, a successful marketing program requires strong strategies for product, promotion, price and place. But, perhaps most importantly, it needs a creative, aggressive and patient sales person who is a combination hunter, teacher, friend, closer and servicer. High-value sales transactions require marketers who have in-depth customer knowledge and the capacity to guide a decision-maker to a satisfactory close over a protracted sales cycle.

Needless to say, over the years, many successful marketing techniques have been developed and deployed to enhance sales professionals' effectiveness. It's a good bet that there have been more books published on "successful selling" than on any other business topic. A very helpful one is <u>Spin Selling</u> in which Neil Rackham advocates a process of "relationship marketing."

His approach is reinforced in another useful marketing textbook, <u>Marketing: Connecting with Customers</u>. In it, Professors Gilbert Harrel and Greg Frazier define relationship marketing as "the development of relational exchanges......*interactive, ongoing, two-way* connections among customers......and other parties for *mutual benefit*." The characteristics underlined in this definition are critical and distinguish this form of marketing from the more commonplace "transactional marketing" which focuses on interaction for a *one-time* transfer of value.

While transactional marketing involves a single event that is "pushed" over a short time frame from the vendor side of the exchange, relationship marketing requires two-way interaction over a much longer period of time. It is concerned with creating an enduring connection that creates value for both parties. The establishment and maintenance of such a "bridge for exchange" requires a great deal of mutual understanding, bred of a long history of meaningful communication.

A link of this nature is extremely important today, given the growing complexity of product and service utilities and the rapid pace of change in our marketplaces. More and more, vendors have to depend on customer loyalty, and customers must rely on trust in their vendors. But this kind of affiliation thrives only if there is a personal bond that is the result of familiarity and long-term, consistent, favorable experience.

Ironically, these were the kinds of connections that prevailed in most of economic history. Until the industrial revolution, vendors and customers knew each other intimately. The client specified his or her need directly to the provider, and the provider custom-fabricated an item or service specifically for the client. It was a face-to-face exchange that involved all vendors, from cobblers to cabinetmakers.

However, as the productive process became more elaborate and automated, layers of other involved parties—and related technology—intervened and separated the craftsman from the consumer. Transactions became more impersonal. Still, the process worked well for generations.

During the first half of the twentieth century, relatively "standardized" products changed little, and customers enjoyed dependable access to them. The "human touch" of a vendor became less important. Since very little changed over time, customers thoroughly understood the product and could count on a simple, consistent, albeit impersonal, system of manufacture and distribution to get it to them reliably.

However, as we began to move through the second half of the twentieth century, product and service innovation, sparked by fresh knowledge-based technology, began to generate a torrent of new, highly differentiated goods and services. Business customers had to struggle to understand the myriad of features, utilities and applications that were offered them, while at the same time striving to understand their own customers' new needs and demands. Moreover, a torrent of new competitors began to invade their marketplace.

Business buyers began to live at a "dog year" pace. It was virtually impossible for them to maintain a real-time knowledge of the relative benefits offered by the army of vendors that was targeting their purchasing budgets. As a consequence, buyers were forced to act on less than perfect knowledge when it came to purchases of complex or "big ticket" goods and services. In these higher risk circumstances, they began to look to vendors with whom they had established a trusting relationship and from whom they could get helpful assistance in making the many decisions that confronted them. The old model of "face-to-face"—or, at least, in this era of advanced communication technology, "virtual face-to-face"—contact became important once again.

As a result, commercial customers are now increasingly looking for vendors who are partners as well as providers. They prefer to deal with people who are willing to take the time to understand the unique nature of their enterprises, people who demonstrate a genuine concern for their success.

Brass Tacks Tip: Successful marketing in this milieu depends on building and maintaining sound, enduring, meaningful, personal relationships, both with existing customers and prospective customers.

RELATE FOR RESULTS

That which grows fast, withers as rapidly. That which grows slowly, endures.

—Josiah Gilbert Holland, Historian

Business-to-business marketers need meaningful, enduring "connections" when dealing with both existing clients and prospects.

Q. In a previous column you talked about the importance of long-term, personal relationships when endeavoring to sell big-ticket items to business customers. Is that what I see touted these days as customer relationship marketing?

A. Yes. And CRM is one of the most important responsibilities of a business owner.

In the case of existing customers, it's important to remember that they are always some other vendors' prospects. A study by SatMetrix Systems has shown that the average firm loses fifty-percent of its customers every five years! Therefore, ongoing communication is essential in order to maintain favorable "top of the mind" awareness within this constituency.

This entails repetitive, meaningful contact. Research shows that most people will retain a material recollection of communication for about six weeks. As a consequence, in order for a vendor to engender consistent, uninterrupted awareness, the client must be contacted at least eight times a year.

Moreover, these contacts should consist of more than a mailed brochure or a mass media advertisement. A worthwhile relationship has to be built on systematic, personalized, consistent intercourse that is uniquely beneficial for the client. Where customers are business owners and CEO's, vendor contacts must be truly helpful.

Busy customers have limited time and short attention spans so, if a vendor is going to impact them favorably, its periodic contacts have to provide a distinct, tangible benefit to the client. Of course, the vendor/ client communication at the time of contact can be wrapped in a subtle underlying sales message, but that marketing message must not over-whelm the primary objective of the contact, i.e. providing an immedi-ate benefit of value to the client, irrespective of that client's readiness to "buy."

In many commercial marketing efforts of this type, vendors convey "gifts" or advertising specialties that are of special value and are tailored to the circumstance. Increasingly, in today's fast-paced, complex world, these are taking the form of actionable information that can be effectively used by the client in the conduct of his or her business affairs. Vendors often provide books, audiotapes, CDs or clippings with on-point information. Sometimes they sponsor seminars, work-shops or networking clinics to which clients are invited.

The informational or educational content conveyed through these "offerings" is structured to provide an easily perceived benefit for the client's firm or for him personally. Such content has to be formulated in a way that is respectful of the receivers' interests, habits and time constraints. It must be devoid of "fluff" and patronization and provide truly substantive insights and assistance.

The subliminal marketing messages it projects, if any, should con-vey—in addition to factual information about products or services—a clear understanding of the positive values and standards embraced by the vendor. If tastefully packaged, this type of material can include a very subtle marketing message.

These offerings should be identified with a specific marketing or ser-vice contact person on the vendor's staff in order to build familiarity and establish a lasting, personal connection. Indeed, this form of client assistance is most effective if it is offered personally, through one-on-one meetings between customer and vendor.

Vendors who employ relationship-marketing techniques commonly supplement their in-person visits that are client initiated (usually involving requests for product or service information or quotes) with one or two unilateral outreach calls per year. Generally, these latter calls include, in addition to a carefully crafted and sensitive marketing pitch, a request for feedback about the client's satisfaction with the impersonal "touches" or "gifts" included in the ongoing contact program. (In fact, this request for feedback can be the premise for an in-person call.)

A properly serviced client will appreciate this kind of vendor professionalism and concern and, thus, be favorably sensitized to the vendor's direct selling approaches. That's why a formal relationship marketing program must be carefully integrated with the marketing and sales programs conducted by a firm's field and in-house sales teams.

Relationship building with prospects is equally important. These days, it takes about twelve contacts with a prospect to consummate a large-ticket sale (compared with only four or five contacts 25 years ago). In cases where the prospect has little awareness of the vendor, even more contacts may be necessary in order to develop familiarity and confidence.

Often, a salesperson will determine during cold calls or early contacts with a prospect that it is, at that time, inappropriate to push to a sale. In these cases, the relationship marketing contact program described earlier can be used to engage the prospect in a comfortable, rewarding "loop" of unconditional involvement, while the marketer searches for a new approach and picks a more propitious time for the next viable step in the selling process. This allows the vendor to "stay in touch" in a manner that will eventually evoke either a client-initiated contact or a more welcome re-contact by the vendor.

A good salesman knows that "no" does not mean "no forever." Circumstances or timing might not be right to consummate a sale at a given point in time. But the involvement of the prospect in a formal, not-yet-transaction-ready relationship can be a commodious "foot-in-the-door" approach that prevents the vendor from "being out of sight; out of mind"......and out of luck.

Brass Tacks Tip: This type of relationship marketing program requires a database that indicates the interests, state of readiness and "hot buttons" of each key decision-maker within client and prospect firms.

TRACK YOUR CUSTOMERS

Knowledge is power.

—Francis Bacon, Philosopher

One only has to read the newspaper to see how rapidly the world of business is changing. New tools and techniques are being introduced daily to help managers cope, and those responsible for running businesses must make continuing, deliberate efforts to understand and exploit these changes for the benefit of their firms.

Q. I've read that "database" marketing is a new and powerful weapon that will change dramatically the way things are sold. How does this work, and can it be of any use to a small firm like mine?

A. Definitions abound for this important marketing technique, but essentially it's a means of identifying and communicating directly with your highest-potential customers. By using rather simple computer technology, critical information about your existing and potential customers can be analyzed to facilitate selection of the prime candidates for your product or service. The same technology then helps you deliver your "pitch" to them, via personal sales calls, mail, telemarketing, or carefully selected mass media.

By knowing exactly whom it is you want to reach, you can preclude expensive overreach and overkill in the marketplace. Resources and energies can be concentrated on those targets that mean the most to your firm.

A good customer information management system will help you keep track of your "rifle shot" marketing efforts and will enable you to compile a history of your relationship with each customer. This trove of information will be invaluable over the long run since it will facilitate an informed, continuing, in-depth relationship with each prime customer.

The low cost, personalized customer contacts that this technique facilitates are ideal for a small business with a limited budget and a need to develop a unique rapport with its clients. Indeed, many experts claim the days of mass media are numbered. High costs, new "narrowcast" media like cable television and the Internet, and the need to overcome "product similarity" with "vendor uniqueness" are prompting even large companies to adopt this tailored, highly focused, very personal approach to selling.

The trick is to gain familiarity with a flexible database software package for your PC. There are many user-friendly versions available today and a computer service company that specializes in small business can give you a jump-start, if necessary. This is not rocket science, and a few nights tinkering with your computer will get you up and running.

Obviously, the most critical component is the customer information that constitutes your base of data. Accumulation of relevant data takes time and effort, but once it is in your electronic box, it's yours to use—and update—forever. Sales records; salesmen's contact reports; customer letters of praise, complaint or inquiry; questionnaire and survey results; directories; newspaper and trade magazine stories; and purchased prospect lists can all provide you with information for your electronic file. It takes discipline to acquire, but once stored, it can be massaged, manipulated and used to give you a powerful, relevant, effective—perhaps exclusive—link to the people and businesses that have the greatest influence on your success.

My ol' uncle Ollie used to say: "It's not what you know; it's who you know." Today, "how you know them" counts, too.

HELP THEM UNDERSTAND

Whether you are really right or not doesn't matter; it's the belief that counts.

—Robertson Davies, Novelist

"Rule #1: The customer is always right."

"Rule #2: If you think the customer is wrong, re-read rule #1."

Q. Most of the positions in my company are entry-level jobs. Only a few of my employees have had experience dealing with demanding customers. How do I convince them that the "customer is always right?"

A. Customer sensitivity is a must in every business, of course. But, give some thought to experimenting with an approach in which you admit that the guy on the other end of the transaction ISN'T always right.

A great deal of employee resistance to the *TCIAR* mantra stems from the fact that many times an intelligent worker can see, firsthand, that the customer is actually wrong......and occasionally, even a first-class jerk! Efforts to convince these employees to the contrary are generally futile. In fact, in extreme cases, workers have been known to go out of their way to prove the moronic nature of their clients.

Also, by insisting that your employees see "the emperor's new clothes" and ignoring the true difficulty of some contemporary customer relationships, you'll contribute a lot of unnecessary stress to your employees' daily routines. Well-placed empathy can work wonders.

By acknowledging the foibles and faults of your customers, you will gain the attention and respect of your workers. However, in these situations, you have to emphasize that, while the customer may be wrong, and while we all may know it, we still have to treat the customer as if he or she were chugging on all cylinders.

The need to foster illusions has been part of the retail process since the time of ancient bazaars. We all strive to make our products and services look great and affordable, even when they fall a tad short of the mark. So, too, must we work to make the personal sales and service functions as attractive, seamless, comfortable and supportive as possible......even if the buyer on the other end is downright demented.

Your employees have to understand that the key to success in your business—and in their careers—is the ability to make every customer—even those offering tough-talk or tantrums—feel right, even when they are not. Your employees don't have to believe it, as long as they make the customer feel it.

Workers should be allowed to make reasonable, personal judgments about a customer, as long as the customer is still treated with the kind of quality care that is the standard of your company. Indeed, constructing an accurate profile of a customer will enable a professional sales or service employee to custom-tailor the attention he or she provides. It's OK to keep an open mind, as long as the mouth stays shut.

BE QUICK TO COLLECT

Man who waits for roast duck to fly into mouth must wait very, very long time.

—Chinese Proverb

Cash is the essential nutrient of any enterprise. Therefore, it's important that it be harvested as soon as possible after a sale is made.

Q. In a previous column you traced a firm's cash shortfall problem to its collection practices. I'm fairly diligent when it comes to collecting my bills, but, try as I may, I always seem to be behind the eight ball when it comes to balancing "cash in" with "cash out." Any tips???

A. While it's always more exhilarating to "sell," a sale is nothing more than a bookkeeping entry until the buyer's cash is in hand. The real positive bottom line impact comes from collecting the proceeds of a sale quickly so that you have the cash to use—to create new inventory, to pay down debt or to acquire a new company asset.

Unfortunately, while most customers will eventually pay what they owe, it generally happens on <u>their</u> schedules. Since it's your schedule of operations that determines <u>your</u> cash needs, you must be proactive in getting your customers to pay up in a manner that appropriately complements your internal cash flow needs. As my ol' uncle Ollie used to say, "Getting paid is good; but getting paid quickly is what it's all about."

If you've got a sizeable slug of receivables that are thirty days old, or any that are riper than forty-five days, your collection mechanics need some fine-tuning.

Here are a few *Brass Tacks Tips* for accelerating your collections:

- Send out invoices immediately after goods are shipped or service provided (and include postage paid return envelope). Send another invoice two weeks later if payment hasn't been received. Also, maintain a strict bi-weekly schedule for sending out "late notices." (Don't give this job to an entry-level drone; we're talking about your money here!)

- You and your designated A/R enforcer should get a weekly report that graphically highlights the status of outstanding receivables and flags slowpays for immediate contact. Make sure the warning bells chime after thirty days and clang after forty-five.

- The collection process should look like a personal quest, not a computer-generated round of "voice-mail-tag." Forget form letters. People love to beat a "system;" they're less brave when it comes to dealing one-on-one with a warrior with a cause.

- Unless you have a big, capable staff, allocate at least two hours each week to making personal follow-up phone calls to the folks who are holding your cash hostage. Know what the net contribution of each customer is to your bottom line so you can allocate your time and tact accordingly. Separate the "OK slow pays" (big, regular customers who buy at the right price) from the "NO-NO slow pays" (small, infrequent, low-margin customers). After you get your money, fire the latter group. Never worry about losing a bad customer.

- First call: be understanding but firm, indicating how important cash flow is to the sound operation of your growing enterprise. Never get hostile, (you don't want to goad the payer into proving he's stronger than you are) but make sure that you clearly state what—and when—your subsequent actions will be if your first call doesn't produce immediate results. (This, of course, requires a well-conceived plan of action—something that should be in place before you dial the phone). Stifle the small talk and try to sound like a professional with a definite plan and timetable. Don't sound desperate: the payer might assume you're not long for this world and try to wait you out. Hold the collection agency/lawyer warnings for the second call or later. Learn to be effective as both Jeykll and Hyde—playing the right role at the right time. A checklist (not a script) that can be refined with experience can help.

- Make sure you are talking to the right person; one who realizes his or her company has something important at stake—someone who can write a check pronto. Let him know who you are and how important this call is. Record the name and phone number of the person you talk with and keep a dated record of what is agreed to. Better yet, follow up with a letter re-iterating your agreement and, if you sense it will help, copy his or her boss. (Be careful here. Sometimes you can get farther schmoozing the worker bee and not creating another reason for him to deal with his superior. If you handle it right, your contact in Accounts Payable might be more willing to improve your standing on the check schedule than will be his cash-strapped boss who sees every dollar as "his" money).

- Squeeze all the information you can out of each conversation (except reasons why the customer is having a hard time…you've got your own problems). Ol' uncle Ollie claims to have once discovered that the routine practice of one of his clients was to cough up cash only after three collection calls. He says he promptly made two more calls.

- If, after all is said and done, it looks like immediate full payment is a stretch, ask for a specific amount to be paid next week, (get a specific date). Never ask, "Well, how much can you pay?" Structure and execute a formal, written payment plan, complete with payment dates, penalty clauses and incentives.

- Reward those who pay—and penalize those who don't—with discounts or late fees……and enforce your policy.

- Make sure you can put the cash to use as soon as it becomes available. A lock box at your bank is a good tool for reducing the downtime of incoming cash.

- If all else fails, (according to your very firm policy as to how long you are willing to wait) hire a professional and be willing to pay whatever commission is required (fees can go as high as 50%). Less than a quarter of receivables over a year old are ever collected. At this point, you're as concerned as much with principle as with cash. You don't want to be featured as a "patsy" on the "Deadbeats of America" web site.

- Always keep in mind while you are waiting for payment that your firm is acting as a no-cost banker for your customer. Cash costs money, whatever its source. While you are twiddling your thumbs, your slow-pay customer is using your cash, interest-free, to finance his operations and fatten his bottom line. If nothing else motivates you to collect, this thought should.

- Finally, don't continue to sell to someone who isn't paying and has a bad track record with your firm. You don't need the grief and you won't get the money.

    Brass Tacks Tip: Treat collecting like the important job it is. It's the most crucial thing you do after "making" and "selling."

WEAVE A WORTHWHILE WEB

Good enough never is.

—Debbi Fields, Entrepreneur

The power and pervasiveness of the Internet is changing the way business leaders access one of their most important resources—information. Indeed, it's forcing information providers to alter the very nature of their stock in trade.

Q. As the owner of a small business, I am, of course, responsible for its Web site. We try to provide interesting information that will attract both existing and potential customers to our site. I'm beginning to worry, however, that the plethora of information on the Internet leaves no room for me to be sufficiently attractive to surfers. How can I refresh my appeal??

A. No question, information has become a commodity. Thanks to the ubiquitousness of the Web, we all enjoy access to more facts, figures and trivia than ever before. In part, this glut was prompted by the nature and rapid growth of our early Web technology. Pressured Web masters quickly learned that textbook-like dumps of information were the most inexpensive lure with which to attract a clientele.

This trend was abetted by the fact that there are a heck of a lot of people in the world today with things to say. Contemporary communication technology now affords them a conduit through which they can conveniently and inexpensively off-load their "intellectual" output. As a result, the supply of information has expanded faster than the demand for it, and its perceived value has plummeted.

But, times they are a-changing. The Web is less of a novelty today and its patrons are becoming more discriminating and selective, growing more sensitive to the difference between nice-to-see data and need-to-know knowledge. Users are beginning to appreciate what best-selling authors have known for a long time, i.e. there is a big difference between <u>Webster's Dictionary</u> and <u>Gone With The Wind</u>. While both works are comprised of words, it is the manner in which those words are crafted into messages that determines their value to a given constituency.

My ol' uncle Ollie used to say, "cream always rises to the top." Quality, style and manner of presentation will always make a determinative difference and, thanks to info-user aids like search engines and "favorite places," discriminating users are finding and patronizing the most talented, creative, value-conveying information providers. Sophisticated consumers of information are increasingly "self-selecting" and affiliating with those bright wordsmiths who offer quality stuff that's been filtered through experienced, learned, market-sensitive minds. Those who seek quality information do what they have to do to get it, even—God forbid—paying for it. Less discriminating folk—the merely curious "surfers" and the cheapskates—will settle for the easy-to-produce bulk stuff that is inundating the Web today. But even that will change.

As you read this, emerging Web technology is already abetting an upgrade in the quality of the information flow that is facilitated by the Internet. "Gizmos" are now available that allow a talented journeyman provider of quality information and valuable knowledge to be adequately rewarded for his or her efforts. These devices function much like meters, actually charging users for the intellectual property they access or download. As this methodology takes hold, profit-motivated information content providers (and who isn't?) will be induced to improve the quality of their product; and new, even more talented providers will be encouraged to hitch their brains to a keyboard and join—and thus improve—the prevailing roster of Web suppliers.

Your job now is to make sure you are in the ranks of these quality providers. Your content has to be superior to any other Web-based material that is directed at your target market. In the early days of television, people were willing to watch a static test pattern because the technology was new and different. Once the "newness" wore off, people demanded the likes of Milton Berle and Edward R. Murrow. The same transition of tastes has occurred with respect to the Internet. The early adopters of this new technology have become highly sophisticated and, when it comes to information, they want the equivalent of a best seller.

Many web masters are trying to offset their wimpy informational content with color, sound, animation and spiffy graphics. While these attributes are important—in fact, they're on their way to becoming "essentials"—they will not compensate for tired and trite content. A good cover might get you to buy an unknown author's first book. But once you read his work, you "know" him and his talent. If it wasn't satisfying, a glitzy cover on his next work will not easily convince you to waste your time again.

So, don't retreat from the fray. While it is increasingly difficult to stand out in the crowd, you can do it if you are outstanding in your field. You must have unique, "one-of-a-kind," current, relevant, always-changing, "knock your socks off" content. It must be easily accessed, manipulated and applied to a visitor's instant needs. Most importantly, it must help an end user create real value and tangible benefits for himself.

When it comes to content, the Web has moved into a new league. You have to be able to move with it or move out of the way.

KNOW YOUR NUMBERS

The art of being wise is the art of knowing what to overlook.

—William James, Philosopher

Thanks to computers, fiber optics, the Internet and old-fashioned human curiosity, business owners like you are awash in information. As a consequence, you are being forced to discriminate between information that is "nice to know" and that which is essential to performance.

Q. Help! I'm drowning in data and I can't determine which reports are flotsam and which are soon-to-sink jetsam. How can I tell which numbers and which reports are necessary for the profitable operation of my business?

A. There's no universally applicable answer to that question. What you must know about your firm's current performance in order to provide appropriate management direction depends on the nature of your business, its competition, and the markets it serves. It is also conditioned by your personal management style.

Let's face it. Mankind has finally found a commodity—information—whose production promises to forever outstrip consumption. "Data dumps" and "number crunching" have become de rigueur in today's business firms. As a result, you probably have more information at hand than you are capable of productively digesting.

Academics tell us that one edition of a contemporary newspaper contains more information than the entire acquired knowledge of the average citizen living in the seventeenth century.

The challenge today is separating the wheat from the chaff. Not only will non-essential information tend to lead you astray, but its consumption eats up valuable time, thus diverting your attention from the things that truly matter.

In the good old days, entrepreneurs depended on their profit and loss statements to provide a measure of performance. Problem is, in today's frenetic environment, the best opportunities to act have passed by the time financial statements are available. P&L's present a nice historical portrait, but typically they are not capable of prompting the specific actions that must be taken immediately in order to stay competitive.

In every business there is a handful of individual numbers that can be compiled daily—a performance report card—that can give its managers both a sense of company performance and the ability to quickly push the operational "buttons" most important to problem resolution and opportunity exploitation.

To determine which "key numbers" work in your organization, review a week's worth of company activity to see which "results" were most distressing and which most satisfying. Then look back and try to envision what you did (or might have done) on a given day that most affected these outcomes. What prompted your decisions or actions? What information might have triggered different, more rewarding results? What do you regret not knowing? What slate of insights, information or understanding would have most profitably guided your actions during that week?

In other words, be a "Monday morning quarterback." Determine both the plays that were—or could have been—most beneficial for your company. Search out the clues you had (or wish you had) to best accomplish play selection. Try to find the few numbers—three, four, no more than a half dozen—that would have most quickly and accurately guided the formulation of a winning playbook. What five or six numbers were available—or should have been available—on a daily basis to prompt and guide your actions? Sales? Collections? Backorders? Raw materials prices? Competitor's advertising space? Occupancy rate? Orders received? Average time to delivery? Customer waiting time?

Determine which individual numbers—<u>not</u> reports crammed with statistics—give you the best insight and cause for action. Make sure they can be available to you fresh, each day, before you have to make critical decisions. Over time, you'll be able to evaluate the relevance of these numbers and refine them or make substitutions.

When ol' uncle Ollie was a teen-aged usher in a neighborhood theater, the manager would send him across the street to the competition to buy an admission ticket at the beginning and end of each evening. By comparing the ticket numbers, the boss knew the "gate" at the other movie house and, by comparing the features playing, he was able to refine his picture-booking skills to counter the competitor who had the greatest effect on his revenues. This same manager also kept a daily running count on popcorn bags in order to discern the overall trend of total concession sales. He had learned that kernels popped bore a direct relationship to overall sales of refreshments.

Writing in <u>INC Magazine</u>, business-owner Jack Stack tells of a gear manufacturer who wanted to see only one number when he came into the office each morning, i.e. the weight of the gears shipped the day before. Since he knew what he was paying to buy a pound of steel, and could easily factor in all related operating costs, he could gauge—by tracking poundage—how his firm was faring financially on a daily basis. Moreover, he could relate that aggregate number to his break-even point and take action quickly if his contribution to profit began to slump.

Brass Tacks Tip: Choose your numbers and watch them carefully.

PICK YOUR PROBLEMS

Things not worth doing are not worth doing well.

—Ken Blanchard, Author

Sometimes it's a wise idea to let problems "ripen" for a while before deciding which ones are important enough to get your full attention.

Q. In a previous column, you advocated "speed" in the operation of a business. I have found that, sometimes, a "go-slow" approach is the best advice when it comes to tackling everyday, operational problems. If I reacted immediately to every issue that landed on my desk, I'd be lunging in a million different directions and getting nothing done in the process. Do you disagree with moving slowly in these kinds of circumstances?

A. Not necessarily. Sometimes unattended problems simply go away. Napoleon used to open his mail just once a month, claiming that, by then, most of the issues had resolved themselves, and he could then spend adequate time tackling the more critical, intractable ones.

While this approach allows for a concentrated use of time and energy, it also leaves a lot to chance. And nowhere is it written that a potentially business-breaking problem must languish benignly until you get around to treating it. By the time you finally do something, it might very well be too late.

This is not to say, however, that every problem is created equal. The Pareto Principle tells us that 20% of the problems usually cause 80% of the ill effects. The trick is finding which of the challenges confronting you are among the one-fifth that can wreak the greatest havoc. Here's where your "triage" talents can pay off. You have to decide which of the problems are the most threatening and worthy of your immediate attention. This is an essential skill for managers as well as emergency room physicians. Both experience and intuition are needed to perform a meaningful diagnosis. Once the priorities have been sorted, speed is of the essence.

You'll probably find that during the course of your selective treatment of the mega-menaces that confront you, the more minor issues have resolved themselves or someone else has stepped in and fixed them for you.

Also, you should be on guard against "accepting" problems not worthy of your time and attention in the first place. In his hilariously insightful book The One Minute Manager Meets the Monkey, Ken Blanchard finds that most of the problems encountered by managers are brought to them by other people who are unjustifiably trying to unburden themselves. They carry these difficulties on their backs like monkeys, just waiting to transfer the monkey, and the responsibility for its care and feeding, to someone else. So, the next time someone stops by your office, be mindful of the fact they are probably carrying at least one monkey that they are, in all probability, going to attempt to leave with you when they depart. Your job as a manager is to make sure that people care for their own monkeys, and that all of yours are properly fed and cared for.

Blanchard suggests that in large companies an inability to hand-off monkeys to one's subordinates is the reason that many managers are typically running out of time while their staffs are running out of work.

MAKE CASH YOUR KING

Happiness is a positive cash flow.

—Fred Adler, Venture capitalist

Cash, in a consistent and predictable flow, is the fuel that propels every business. Indeed, cash is king, both in new ventures where it's scarce and in established companies that are growing or introducing new, unproven products or services.

Q I operate a relatively new business and my accountant tells me that, at this stage of development, cash flow is more important than profit. What say you???

A In a perfect world, the cash flowing into your coffers would be at least equal to the cash flowing out in any given period of time, and you could devote all of your attention to cranking a profit by year end. But, this isn't a perfect world. Lumps of cash must be expended from time to time for capital equipment, facilities or inventory that won't generate an offsetting inflow of cash immediately. Also, customers aren't generally inclined to pay your invoices on receipt. The products or services you've sold them required an outlay of cash on your part, but you're not going to see cash from your customers for 30, 60 or even 90 days.

As a consequence, you have to carefully and frequently monitor the "ins" and "outs" of greenbacks to ensure that your cash obligations can be adequately satisfied. This means that you have to prepare monthly cash flow projections, at least. Keep in mind, a cash flow statement is every bit as important as a profit and loss statement. In fact, if your firm's cash doesn't flow properly, it may not survive to produce a P&L.

The statements you receive at the end of the year from your accountant are great historical records that will give you some insight relative to the things you did or should have done during the past 365 days. They may give you some guidance for the future, but the only sound way to vouchsafe the important liquidity of your firm over the forthcoming 365 days is to produce a statement of your own forward-looking cash flow anticipations.

Brass Tacks Tip: At the beginning of every year, create a spreadsheet that shows the dollars that you think will actually flow in and out of your business each month for the next twelve-month period. A thirty-six month projection is even better, since it will give you precious lead-time to fix a cash problem that might be lurking down the line.

Obviously, this isn't an easy chore. But it must be done. Every anticipated source of dollar revenue and every probable outlay must be logged into the thirty-day period in which it will occur. This projection enables you to determine how much cash must be available to sustain the level of business you expect. An exercise like this will also prompt you to be more aggressive in collecting your receivables. It might even trigger changes in your pricing and in the arrangements you have with your vendors. Moreover, it will probably cause you to look more critically at your operations with an eye to reducing cash-draining expenses.

Importantly, cash flow data indicate the additional funds that you might have to borrow or otherwise source to sustain the business. In this context, cash flow analyses can help condition your decisions with respect to growth or diversification. As ol' uncle Ollie used to say, "If you don't got the ante, you can't play the game."

Once the year commences, careful, daily monitoring of your cash flow statement will enable you to match performance to plan and to make adjustments accordingly.

Great care should be taken in preparing cash flow projections. When a company is out of cash, it is out of business. A zero or negative cash balance means that payrolls can't be met, materials and inventories can't be paid for, and other critical outlays for things like rent and taxes will be precluded.

Many entrepreneurs are surprised to discover that a successful, rapidly-growing business can present the most severe cash problems. Sales are one thing. But collecting the dollars those sales represent is an entirely different matter. Dollars-in-the-pocket may trail sales by weeks or months. And, in the interim, a successful company's immediate cash obligations will continue to expand. Therefore, accurate, detailed projections of actual "cash in" and actual "cash out" are essential.

Brass Tacks Tip: While there are a lot of "packaged" computer programs available that can help you with this chore, your first attempt to formulate a comprehensive, detailed cash flow projection should be undertaken with a pencil (one with a big eraser) and a large sheet of multi-columned ledger paper. Make each cash entry by hand, and do all the calculations yourself with a small calculator. While this will be relatively slow and painful, it will force you to carefully think through each financial entry, and its implications, as you proceed. After all, it's important that you understand every aspect of the financial flow of your enterprise and that you correct your flawed assumptions and errors as you move along. This laborious paper-and-pencil approach will force you to see the "whole" of your business undertaking and trace through the critical interrelationships of each part.

Once you've sweated over this compilation, you can transfer it to a Lotus or Excel spreadsheet (or something similar) so that you can easily manipulate the data, test "what if" hypotheses, make adjustments based on revised operating tactics, and keep the information up to date. You'll probably have to tinker with the data as you plot a course for your business that is in keeping with the cash you have or are able to source externally. You'll be surprised how this exercise will test your "street smarts" as a business operator.

Brass Tacks Tip: Be cautious in the use of high-powered computer-based spreadsheets in plotting your firm's financial future. The speed and precision of a PC can seduce almost any forecaster into equating its facility for manipulating numbers with accuracy and inevitability. The whiz-bang efficiency of a computer makes it all too easy to believe the numbers it spews forth are predestined. As a consequence, busy business operators often neglect the attention to realistic data entry that is necessary to keep projections practical and relevant.

As ol' uncle Ollie often opined, "Every one of them dang electronic boxes should have a warning label: "garbage in=garbage out."

DON'T FIGHT DILUTION

Nothing is enough to the man for whom enough is too little.

—Epicurus, Greek Philosopher

For a struggling entrepreneur, it's difficult to give anything away…not to mention stock in his or her first-born venture.

Q. Two friends and I started a technology-based company three years ago. It has grown faster than we anticipated and we now find ourselves in need of additional capital. We've tried to borrow money, to no avail. We have found a couple of private investors, but they want a significant amount of our stock in return for the funds they provide. I'm in favor of it, but my two partners say that it is foolish to give stock away now when it is going to be much more valuable in the future. What do you think?

A. If you've exhausted every other source of funding, tell your partners to get with the program. First of all, you are not *giving* the stock away. You are getting a much-needed injection of cash at a time when it could make a significant difference to your company. Here are a few **Brass Tacks Tips** you should give to your partners:

- A company will wither and die if it isn't given the nourishment it needs (i.e. cash) to fuel its growth. In the absence of any other alternative, a private cash-for-stock deal makes perfect sense, assuming that you negotiate for the largest bundle of cash you can get for the stock you are making available. An accountant who is experienced in these kinds of transactions can be of great help in estimating the present and future values of your enterprise. These can be great guideposts in dealing with capital providers.

- The best way to insure that you've got the best deal possible is to engage more than one investor group. If you've got a promising venture, crafty investors will bid to be part of it.

- The highest bidders don't always make the best partners. Make your choice both on the amount of money to be raised and on the "chemistry" you enjoy with the bidders. The investors will be key members of your team for some time to come, so make sure you get into bed with investors who won't give you nightmares.

- Don't dally in making a deal. The longer your search for capital takes, the longer you will have to wait to seize the opportunity you have to grow profitably. Moreover, don't assume an absence of competition. While you search for the absolute best deal, competitors can easily "take the money and run," leaving your firm in the lurch.

- One hundred percent of the equity in an enterprise that is languishing or going down hill isn't worth eighty-percent of a well-capitalized firm that's moving up and out at a brisk, promising clip. The capital you raise by giving up equity will make the difference between having total ownership of a dream or some ownership of a viable business. Every time you pay your electricity bill you are giving up a little bit of the present cash value of your company. But without the juice, where are you? Right. In the dark. The whole process of building a business involves a stream of "give-ups" and "gets." Your job is to make sure the balance between the two is the best you can achieve.

- You should feel flattered that somebody wants a piece of your action. Obviously, your potential investors see a bright future for the combination of your venture and their money. Otherwise, they wouldn't be putting their hard-earned cash on the line. Together you'll make beautiful music if you use the new capital wisely. As a consequence, your piece of the equity will be worth much more in years to come.

- Get over the mindset that "it's my baby and survives and thrives today because of my blood, sweat and tears." You did a great job...so far. But without more of the key resource (which you don't have at present), your baby will never grow up enough to fight the bullies down the block.

- Venture capital ain't cheap. Angel investors typically look for an average annual return of forty percent or more. Of course, you aren't going to pay them that amount each year, but the value of their equity at the time they are ready to cash in, say five years hence, will have to be equated to a cumulative annual gain in the forty-percent-plus range. The interest evidenced by your prospective investors—assuming you told them the truth and nothing but the truth—suggests that they've concluded that such a return is probable. This should make you feel good about the "gets" in your future while you are feeling bad about "give-ups" of the present.

- You have to give serious thought to monetizing your investors' interests down the line. A public offering, a second round of financing, a bank loan or an accumulation of company cash may be needed to take your investors out of the deal a few years from now. The second thing you should do when you get the investors cash is to start planning how you are going to give it back......with sufficient payment for its use. (The first order of business, of course, is putting the newfound cash to good, profitable use.)

- You don't have to give up control of the company. Outside investors don't want to run your business. They have other deals to make. They are putting their money where your mouth is to allow you to run the company and to do it profitably. Do that well, and they won't bother you. Be ready to give up one or more seats on your

Board of Directors, however. They want to know the intimate details of what is happening to their money and the expectations you outlined when you solicited their money. They probably will want a shareholders' agreement that gives them the right to assume control if you do not reach certain benchmarks of performance. These checkpoints should be carefully negotiated prior to closing the deal. Don't let your enthusiasm lock you into performance requirements you can't meet.

Work to get your partners to sincerely buy into the points listed above. Neither you nor your financial partners want to work with sourpuss critics who aren't enthusiastic members of the team.

BEWARE "THE HAND THAT FEEDS"

Be careful what you ask for because you just might get it.

—Source unknown

The typical small business receives about forty percent of its required start-up capital from the founding entrepreneur's family members. But there are some unique problems and pitfalls associated with keeping such financing "all in the family."

Q. I've invested all the liquid funds I can afford in my new machine design and repair business, but just as things are about to take off, I find that I've exhausted my working capital. My father and my brother-in-law have indicated that they might be willing to invest in my company. Is this a good idea?? If so, what's the best way to do it??

A. Many successful companies have been bootstrapped this way, including The Limited Inc., Gateway 2000 Inc., and Walgreen Co. However, there are a number of special precautionary **Brass Tacks Tips** to be attended to when dealing with family members.

- Make sure you are scrupulously candid in your description of the business opportunity and its prospects. Provide as much information as you can about the nature of the enterprise, its anticipated markets, competition, and the trends in the industry. A business plan should be prepared and explained, in detail, to your potential investors.

- Have a firm idea of how much capital you really need and be able to show investors how it will be used. Pro forma profit and loss statements and cash flow projections can be helpful in this regard.

- Don't paint an overly optimistic forecast. Remember that your relatives (especially momma) are inclined to place greater trust and confidence in you than in the typical off-the-street entrepreneur. Because of your blood ties, they'll be inclined to assume that you wouldn't let them get hurt under any circumstances. But business is business, and many start-ups do, unfortunately, come to naught. So make sure that every investor knows the risks involved and of the limitations you will face "making good" if something does go awry.

- Convey realistic expectations to family members. After all, if the business does not do as well as they've hoped, you'll still have a lot of family reunions and Thanksgiving Day dinners to attend, and you don't want to be the turkey that has let them down.

- Take heed of the words of Ricky Ricardo to Lucy: "You gotta lotta splain'in to do." Relatives have more frequent and easy access to you than do outside investors, so they will always want to know what's happening (and to give you the benefit of their advice). Be prepared to spend a lot of time keeping family investors up to date. This is one of the disadvantages of financial help from kinfolk. When disseminating information, even informally, make sure that ALL investors get the same story, especially if some of them are non-relatives. It might be wise to schedule shareholder meetings a couple of times a year to keep them uniformly informed.

- Ensure that all immediate family members of each investor also get information about the venture, its opportunities and its risks. The disgruntled spouses of family members who have invested can be the most retributional in unfortunate circumstances, especially if they had to give up a vacation or a new car because of losses they will undoubtedly attribute to you.

- Be sure to let everyone know what role, if any, they will play in the business. Don't let them perceive themselves as operationally-involved "partners" if that is not what you intend. You must let them know, up front, what you expect and what they can expect. Also, early investors typically don't get dividends in a fledgling venture and certainly cannot expect free lunches, gifts from inventory, reimbursement for travel and the like.

If relatives' contributions are to be investments instead of loans, it will be necessary to incorporate the business and sell them shares of stock. Since there will not be a ready market through which they can liquefy their investment if they need cash, you will want to effect a buy-sell agreement that will specify the means by which you, the firm, or other investors will be able to acquire outstanding shares. This agreement should spell the earliest date at which they will be able to effect a redemption (give yourself plenty of time to get the business cranking), and it should provide a formula for determining the value of the shares in the future.

Importantly, this buy-sell agreement should cover ALL shares outstanding and should allow you or the firm to re-acquire all shares at a formula-determined price at, or after, some point in the future. The formula you use should reflect the true value of the enterprise at any given point in time so that investors will be properly rewarded when they cash in their equity stake.

Your unilateral ability to re-purchase all shares at some future point is critical. Future efforts to re-finance, expand or sell the business will depend on your equity control of the business, and 100% ownership will give you the most options. Such buy-back provisions should not go into effect immediately, however, since you will want to allow for enough time for shareholders to realize reasonable share value appreciation. It might also be wise to include a contract provision that calls for a price floor or price premium in the event of a buy-back.

Brass Tacks Tip: Above all else, make sure you get legal counsel......and document everything in writing.

Don't forget, stock issued early in a venture's life will generally be sold on the cheap. In other words, you will give up more of the company for less money than you will be able to do in the future if the company grows and prospers. This is why, in the early years of an enterprise, many entrepreneurs, like you, will opt for borrowed funds instead of invested-equity capital.

KNOW WHAT IT'S WORTH

Put all your eggs in one basket—and watch that basket.

—Andrew Carnegie, Industrialist

Value, like beauty, is in the eye of the beholder. Similarly, a company's financial value is a function of who is trying to appraise it.

Q. How can I determine how much my business is worth? Does it depend on its sales, the assets it owns, or what? I'd really like to know how much wealth I've created by slaving for over thirty years.

A. To you, your business is priceless. The time and energy you've invested and the other opportunities you've foregone in the pursuit of success entitle you to attach any value you wish to your accomplishments. However, what your company is worth to someone else is another matter. In all probability, a prospective buyer, the IRS, a banker, or an insurance agent would each come up with a different value.

Indeed, the value you finally establish will probably depend on the reason for setting a "price" in the first place. If you want to sell the business, insure it, or use it as collateral, you'll favor a high value. For purposes of calculating your estate tax, gifting shares to family members, or making an acquisition, you'll want as low a value as possible. Accordingly, valuation experts will employ a variety of techniques, depending on the reason they were retained.

Most basic techniques fall into three broad categories. The first looks primarily at the value that the stock market places on similar, publicly-traded companies. This is a favorite approach of the IRS, especially at times when the stock market is at a high. Make a list of public companies that have a SIC (Standard Industrial Classification) number the same as yours. Next, examine the companies on it to find those that have operations, markets and strategies similar to yours. Then check out the current share prices of those companies as a multiple of their earnings per share. Apply those multiples to your firm's earnings, and you'll have some idea of how the IRS might ascribe a value to your company.

This is also a good technique to use if you are contemplating a sale of your business to a public company or if you are making a gift of stock to a charity and want to determine the deduction to which you should be entitled.

This technique actually reflects future prospects since the prices of most public companies take into consideration expected growth and performance.

The problem, obviously, is finding a comparable company that "fits" your firm's profile. A stodgy firm with limited growth potential might warrant a multiple of two to six times earnings. A solid company with good prospects might sell today for a factor of fifteen to fifty. A "hot" venture in communications or computer technology might demand a triple digit P/E ratio. But, remember, these are public companies. The value of your firm will probably be significantly less since its equity shares are not easily sold and liquefied.

Another approach looks at the current market value of the net assets utilized by a business. An appraisal establishes the value of the real property, plant and equipment and existing inventory of the enterprise. From that, all outstanding debts and obligations are deducted. The surplus of assets over liabilities is the value. This is a very crude approach that is used primarily in situations where a company has a substantial asset base that is producing insubstantial income. In other words, the company is probably worth more dead than alive, and the owner's best option for realizing value is liquidation of the assets. An exception to this scenario is the company that owns valuable intangible property like patents, trademarks or hard-to-duplicate customer good-will. In these circumstances, the value of these marketable assets—that typically do not appear on the balance sheet—must be estimated and added to the calculated surplus.

Perhaps the most popular approach to valuation involves "discounted cash flow." It is based on the premise that a profit-motivated buyer will have the final word on the value of your enterprise. Since a buyer will invest money only if a return is probable, the amount of that projected return over future years will determine how much money an acquirer will put up today to realize it. The "present value" of those future returns will approximate the highest price a buyer will offer.

This makes a lot of sense. If someone is going to buy a business for, let's say, $200,000, he or she will want to realize annual income from that investment in an amount greater than he would be able to obtain from a savings account, corporate bonds, or mutual fund, all of which are less risky and more liquid than the company they are buying. It's not unreasonable to be seeking a 15%-20% return on one's money or, in the case of this business, $30,000 or $40,000 a year. And, if one plans on working in the business, this return should be above and beyond a reasonable salary for one's efforts.

Therefore, a sophisticated buyer of a business typically attempts to determine the stream of "free cash flow" that will be produced by the firm over a period of years. This is the flow of annual earnings, after tax, to which already-expensed depreciation is re-added and from which the amount of capital outlays needed to maintain ongoing operations is deducted. This stream of future returns is then discounted by an interest rate factor that reflects the potential return from alternative investments and the risk involved in this particular venture. Also added to this stream of operating flows is the discounted value of the estimated price that the firm will fetch when it is sold again in the future by the new buyer. The result is a "present value" that an interested purchaser would probably assign to the potential acquisition. Most spread sheet software will allow you to easily calculate the present value from a sequence of cash flows. The real challenge is to accurately forecast what those flows will be.

Whatever the reason for your desire to establish value, I strongly suggest you retain the services of an experienced accountant or business valuation specialist. A book like Shannon Pratt's <u>Valuing a Business</u> (Richard D. Irwin & Co.) could help greatly.

BE PREPARED

Better is half a loaf than no bread.

—John Heywood, Writer

Most businesses are "family businesses," meaning that more than one member of a family is involved in the ownership or operation of the firm. But even when there is no day-to-day direct involvement of a family in the affairs of a business, family concerns and considerations often affect decisions that are made with respect to the company.

Q. My last marriage ended in divorce, and the fight over my business left me with little more than half the ownership and no incentive to make it profitable. Result: the business disappeared. I started a new business—now very successful—and am about to marry again. How do I prevent a repeat but still be fair to her?

A. Before you walk down the aisle, see a good matrimonial lawyer about a prenuptial agreement. While laws vary from state to state and there is no guarantee that a pre-nup will stand the stress of a bitter divorce, full disclosure and free acceptance by both parties at the time of execution can allow such an agreement to minimize the financial damage to both parties—and the business—before a problem erupts.

Prior to executing such an agreement, you should get a professional evaluation of your firm's worth and establish a jointly acceptable method for valuing its shares in the future. Also, you might consider using the pre-nup, a separate buy/sell agreement, or a restrictive legend on the stock shares, to retain a right—with reasonable and fair terms—for you or your firm to buy back any equity that a divorce decree could put in the hands of your spouse. This kind of control will promote stability and facilitate profitable continuity of the business while still allowing the departing spouse to get a fair share of monetized equity.

These are ticklish issues to tackle in a period of pre-marital bliss, but it's in the interests of both parties to avoid breaking the connubial golden eggs that, with care and foresight, their corporate "goose" can provide to each for years to come.

Depending on the size and viability of your business, you might also consider an ESOP. An employee stock ownership program would allow a trust established for the benefit of your employees to purchase your spouse's stock for cash. This approach would give her spendable/investable dollars, would provide your workforce with a motivating benefit, and would allow you to keep control of the firm. Depending on the financial condition of your firm, a leveraged ESOP—funded with borrowed funds—might be a beneficial approach. Also, if you and your spouse can agree on an equitable financial arrangement before your divorce is final, you could gift her shares of stock as part of your settlement while you are still married—tax free since she is your spouse—and she could sell the shares to the ESOP after the divorce. Significant tax benefits are available to the seller of company stock through an ESOP, and a reduction in the amount due Uncle Sam could mean a less financially painful separation for you and your spouse. Check out the suitability of this technique with your attorney and accountant. It might benefit all involved parties.

WATCH OUT FOR THE SLIPPERY SLIDE

*When a feller gits a goin down hil, it dus seem as tho evry thing has
bin greased for the okashun.*

—Josh Billings, Essayist

While the failure rate for businesses is nowhere near the eighty-percent
number bandied about by "chicken little" pessimists, the sad fact is
that no enterprise, large or small, has a natural immunity to failure.

Q. I started my own business almost five years ago. While I never set
the world on fire, I was able to meet my payroll, satisfy my creditors
and pay myself a decent salary. Lately, however, I've had a queasy feeling that things are "unraveling." I still enjoy moderately good sales, but
cash is hard to come by, and this could be a loss year. How can I tell if
I am on that proverbial "slippery slide" to oblivion?

A. You are at a point in time where this is a difficult call to make.
The business is still young enough to be suffering the typical "ups" and
"downs" that plague start-ups. The old "feast or famine" syndrome
tends to hang on in some businesses, but by no means is it a clear bell-
wether of failure.

That is not to say, however, that you shouldn't be concerned. If
your bookkeeper is frowning more than usual, if you've had to dip into
your pocket frequently to meet a payroll, or if the big customer you
were sure would come through just took a raincheck, it would be wise
to do an operational "reality check."

Sit down with your accountant and get an exact fix on your firm's
present financial condition. Income statements and balance sheets that

are six months old won't help. You need sales and cash flow information that is current.

Try to decipher relevant trends in sales. Are your "steady" customers still consistent? Where are new sales, if any, coming from? Are you maintaining an adequate gross margin between your revenues and your cost of sales? Is the margin adequate to cover your routine expenses? Examine your sales cycle to see if it is taking too long to move from an initial customer contact to the receipt of an order. Is it taking too long to collect on your invoices?

Focus on those customer segments that are the most responsive and contribute the greatest amount to total sales and to your margins. Keep in mind the "Pareto Principle" suggests that eighty percent of your sales come from twenty percent of your customers.

Also, revisit your break-even point to see if you are achieving the volumes necessary—in every line of business—to support your operation. If not, you might have to consider trimming your product or service lines to a core that that gives you the biggest bang for the buck. Some serious reduction in costs and expenses might also be warranted. Are you buying at the best price? Do you really need everything you are paying for?

In addition, examine your own pricing policies. Are they in line with your break-even point and your competitors' prices? What's the price elasticity of your prime market? Maybe you're not charging as much as customers are willing to pay.

Put together an aged payables list to see how much you owe and to whom you owe it. Be particularly scrupulous with respect to payroll taxes and sales taxes for which you might be personally liable. Make sure you haven't been getting a free—apparently profitable—ride by ignoring your vendors or suppliers.

Be sure that you have the right employees doing the right jobs and that they are organized, supported and motivated to provide the kind of productivity you need. Staff realignments or reductions might be necessary. Rank your employees according to their essentiality, productivity and overall performance. Aside from being your most important resource, your employees are generally your largest and most manageable expense.

Get a handle on your cash. Start a daily cash flow log to determine just where your cash is coming from and where it's going. Are your "sources" of cash adequate and your "uses" of it appropriate? Get on top of your receivables. Are you collecting quickly enough? Making sales is one thing; getting the cash in hand is another. Customers who don't pay are more damaging than prospects who don't buy. Remember, "cash is king," and sometimes it's wise to "fire" a customer.

Gather the troops together and brainstorm your situation. Structure the meeting on a positive note. No one likes to be part of a "losing" team, so communicate with your employees like an optimistic "winner." Your business problems are yours and won't be lessened by "dumping" them on your team members. Nevertheless, see if you can jointly develop some strategies for operational improvement. Workers closest to the daily operations and to your customers generally have the best view of what's happening and why. They also can be your best source of ideas for constructive change. But, keep in mind, you have to ask for their help and be seriously interested in what they have to say. It's quite possible that one or two major things—like a machine configuration, collection procedure or price—can be changed quickly to produce significant, immediate results.

Finally, you might want to apply the "Z-Score Calculation" that was presented almost twenty years ago in the Corporate Controller's and Treasurer's Report. It suggests that if your firm has a Z Score of less than 1.81, you have a high probability of failing within two years. Simply calculate the following five financial ratios, multiply by the weights indicated, and total the results: Working capital as a percent of assets times 1.2, PLUS retained earnings as a percent of assets times 1.2, PLUS pretax income plus interest as a percent of assets times 3.3, PLUS sales divided by assets times 1.0, PLUS book value of your stock times .6.

While no formula can be totally predictive, this one might give you a helpful "heads up."

NEVER(?) SAY DIE

If at first you don't succeed, try, try and try again. Then give up.
There's no use being a damn fool about it.

—W.C. Fields, Humorist

Business owners never like to throw in the towel. But, on occasion, that can be the right course of action.

Q. I've been struggling with my business for three years and still haven't made a penny of profit beyond my small salary. How can I tell whether it's time to give up and move on?

A. The typical business gets started and survives because its founder doesn't know the meaning of the word "quit." Absolute conviction and commitment are essential. Anything less and an entrepreneur's chances for success drop to nil.

But unswerving dedication to a goal is warranted only if the cause is truly worthy. That's why a business idea must be scrupulously evaluated before any attempt is made to commercialize it. You could work fruitlessly for a lifetime trying to convert a bad idea to a marketable product.

Assuming a good concept at the beginning, an entrepreneur usually has to give it his all for three to five years. Most new firms don't produce a profit in their early years. I've seen some venturers go for ten years without a reasonable return because they believed in—and enjoyed—what they were doing. In my opinion, there can be no second-guessing whatsoever for at least three years.

For the next two years you should keep the same confidence level but do some careful, limited analysis to determine whether fine-tuning is necessary. If your profits and prospects haven't changed after five years, give your concept, strategy and tactics a very thorough examination. Make sure your opportunity hasn't turned into an obsession. As Kenny Rodgers advises, you have to "know when to hold 'em and know when to fold 'em."

GET READY, GET SET......GO!

Destiny is not a matter of chance, it is a matter of choice; it is not a thing to be waited for, it is a thing to be achieved.

—William Jennings Bryan, Orator

"Hell no, I won't go!" was the rallying cry among draft-age youth during the Vietnam War era. Today, it's the mantra of many business owners who, even at a point in life blessed by advanced age, health and wealth, don't want to give up control of their companies. This, of course, makes it tough on family members and key employees who are understandably anxious to assume the helms of these firms and "do it their way." It's also distressing for the millions of employees of family businesses and closely-held firms who wait daily for a proverbial "shoe" to drop. (Family businesses represent more than seventy-five percent of all business enterprises.)

Q. I'm a foreman of a plant owned by a 79-year-old man who refuses to turn over the shop to his 53-year-old "kid." In the meantime we are missing many opportunities and no one is sure of what the future holds. How do we get him to see the light?

A. The uncertainty and unpredictability of such a situation is tough on loyal followers who want the best for a firm and their future with it. But this is a common conundrum. Owners—even octogenarians—can recite a litany of reasons why the time isn't right. "My health is excellent." "Talented successors are hard to find." "The taxes would kill me." "We are at a critical point in our history, and no one can do this job as well as I." "I don't want to choose one person and disappoint many."

The truth of the matter is that, over time, a business becomes its owner's soulmate and lover, and it takes some pretty powerful reasons for him or her to leave it. Many owners fear that taking leave of their enterprises would result in a loss of identity, social position, and relevance. They dread endless, empty hours bereft of contact with customers and cronies. Not a pretty prospect for someone who spent most of his or her life caring for and feeding a demanding "lover."

On the other hand, the up-and-comers have some good arguments for putting the old horse out to pasture. Every firm needs a constant flow of new ideas and energy. Young successor stallions thrive on opportunities to take more risk, do more, and make more. They need to feel a sense of personal progress; they covet opportunities to show what they can do. Increasingly, they crave a piece of the action.

So, who is right? Who should prevail? The answer is everybody, although the owner has the catbird seat since "possession is nine-tenths of the law." But an owner must be mindful of the fact that with ultimate control comes the ultimate responsibility for the welfare of the firm and all of its constituents. A successful owner has created a value that is extremely important to employees, vendors, customers, family members and the communities touched by his or her firm's operations. No matter what pocket holds this treasure, the owner has a responsibility to protect and vouchsafe it.

The good news is that the owner can "have his cake and eat it, too" if he is willing to make some preparations. The quid pro quo can be palatable: Keep the top spot but make some specific contingency plans. The goal of such planning does not have to be the "graduation" of the owner at a definite point in time. For all the reasons mentioned, an owner might prefer to hold off succession until his age and blood pressure approach triple digits....or until he is hit by that proverbial big red truck. But whatever the owner's present intentions, a comprehensive contingency succession plan must be in place for the benefit of all. In every life—even that of a hale and hearty business owner—the "if" always becomes a "when." If an owner ignores this fact and the preparations it begs, he threatens his legacy and the inheritances of all those touched by the business.

A contingency plan should:

- Identify and prepare successors to both ownership and management positions.

- Let key employees know just what will happen and who will be affected when a transition finally occurs (uncertainty in this regard hurts productivity and might even cause some essential players to jump ship in the interim).

- Provide for funding to facilitate a change in ownership. A well structured insurance program with inexpensive, properly-owned life and disability insurance will provide both the purchase wherewithal for the eventual successors and the deserved financial rewards for the seller and his or her family.

- Contain a will, estate plan, buy/sell agreements and shareholder agreements that allow everything to eventually happen without a hitch.

- Include a tax plan and equity distribution scheme that reduces to a minimum the eventual take of every firm's big "silent partner," Uncle Sam.

- Provide for an appropriate, up-to-date corporate charter, bylaws, minute book and stock certificates.

- Establish ownership structure that protects the business wealth from frivolous litigation and claims.

- Take care of family members who will not be involved in the business once the owner moves on.

- Make provisions for a stock gifting program that allows the owner to effect a tax-advantaged distribution of equity without relinquishing control.

Brass Tacks Tip: A business owner must, early on, organize his attorney, accountant, insurance provider and financial planner into a proactive team with definite marching orders. Their work product should be a carefully designed succession plan, contingent in nature if that is the wish of the owner. This is literally a life and death issue since, in these kinds of circumstances, the dreaded "if" always becomes a "when."

CASH IN CREATIVELY

These guys don't write you a check just for wearing the right tie.

—Joseph Parella, Investment banker

The most valuable asset in almost every entrepreneur's portfolio is the enterprise he or she has created. But it's not always easy to convert that asset into cold, hard cash.

Q. I've built a successful business that provides marketing services to other firms. Most of my personal wealth is tied up in the corporation. I followed your suggestions for establishing a value for my firm, but my accountant says I may be too optimistic. He claims service firms are generally worth less than similar size manufacturing or trade businesses. Is that true?

A. Unfortunately, service businesses, by and large, are less valuable in the market than businesses that make products or merchandise goods and services. This is primarily due to the fact that your firm's principal assets—especially you—go home every night at quittin' time.

Unless your firm employs extensive, expensive technology to facilitate the process by which your employees convey value to your clients, the majority of the true worth of your company consists of you and the employees who work for you. Therefore, a potential buyer of your business is not going to pay you very much for the right to hire people he might be able to otherwise attract in the open market at no up-front cost.

Indeed, your key employees might very well decide to start their own business when you decide to cash it in. (Let's hope they don't get the entrepreneurial itch <u>before</u> you decide to call it quits. My ol' uncle Ollie claims that "Every saloon owner's bartender is his next new competitor.")

The unique talents you bring to your enterprise, the personal contacts you have with clients, your reputation, and your industriousness are personal and intangible and can't be sold to another aspiring, entrepreneur. Worst case, your business is worth the furniture, computers and real estate that support your present employees. And these tangibles can easily be purchased—at no premium—from sources other than you.

Now the good news. There are some things you can do to build the value of the intangible, marketable "goodwill" in your business. As the worth of your goodwill increases, so will the price that you can command from a potential buyer. Here are some ***Brass Tacks Tips:***

First, try to grow your business to a size that will be difficult for someone else to replicate. Proprietary operating systems and procedures, computer software, trademarks and copyrights, and brand names will add unique value to your firm. Contractual agreements with your most important customers can be worthwhile assets too, providing your clients don't demand an "escape clause" that can be triggered in the event of your departure. Employment contracts with key personnel can also help, although, to be enforceable, they cannot be too restrictive.

It's also possible to sell ownership interests to your key employees well in advance of any significant move on your part. Not only will some employee ownership increase your firm's present productivity, but it can also help facilitate their purchase of your majority interest when you decide its time to move on, whether it's retirement that beckons or a new frontier. (Remember, your employees will probably be willing to pay more for your firm than will someone who is not familiar with the business. Often, owner-employees will pay a premium to gain control and to obviate the possible need to find another job when a new owner takes over.) Don't overlook the possibility of an ESOP, which is a tax-advantaged employee stock ownership plan.

When the time comes, you might also want to explore the possibility of selling out to a "roll-up" acquirer, a new type of "conglomerator" that has emerged during the past decade. These acquirers employ "platform investing" or "leveraged buildup" techniques to aggregate and "roll up" small, local or regional service companies into large enterprises with national or super-regional presence. All manner of hitherto "mom and pop" shops are being rolled into national powerhouses, including: funeral homes, investment management advisors, overnight package delivery services, golf resorts and health clubs, animal hospitals and kennels, junkyards and scrap processors, temporary employment agencies, uniform rental services, landfill sites, heating and air-conditioning suppliers, automobile dealers and physician group practices.

The transaction methodology that births these ventures is rather simple. The initial investors usually buy a service firm with $10 to $15 million in annual revenue. This company then becomes the "platform" to which other acquired companies can be added. The new acquisitions are often accomplished with a combination of cash and notes or restricted stock in the platform company. Typically, there is an agreement with each seller to pay down the notes, buy back the stock associated with the transaction, or exchange the stock for negotiable securities once a public offering of the amalgamated enterprise is accomplished. It is anticipated—but not guaranteed—that the augmented platform company will seek to do a public offering once its revenues hit the magic $100 million plateau. At that future point, all participants get cash and marketable securities. In the meantime, the consolidated enterprise profits—it is hoped—from economies of scale, elimination of administrative redundancy, pooled marketing and added leverage.

If executed properly, this technique can benefit everyone involved. A business owner can "monetize" his or her life's work by selling it at earnings multiples that far exceed those achievable via a sale of a service business to another local entrepreneur; key employees get to grow with a dynamic national business; and investors/acquirers can use the leverage and securities of a public company to accomplish tax-advantaged transactions. Last but not least, as the new "roll-up/IPO's" come to market, private investors have an opportunity to invest in types of service enterprises that were previously not open to them.

It's important, however, for a business owner to make sure he's selling out to a financially sound and well run enterprise, especially if he is taking back stock or agreeing to a long-term cash pay-out. One major player in the funeral services business recently stumbled badly, placing in jeopardy the future contingent payments to sellers who had been "rolled up."

Moreover, all businesses are not good candidates for this kind of amalgamation. Experience has shown that enterprises like restaurants, beauty shops, dry cleaners and auto repair businesses don't thrive with centralized management. Industry segments that prosper only when the operating entrepreneur has hands-on control and continuing intimate contact with customers are the least likely to benefit from "nationalization." But the jury is still out. Who would have thought that the barber I grew bald with would be replaced by somebody called Fantastic Sam?

RECRUIT THE HELP YOU NEED

People seldom improve when they have no model but themselves to copy after.

—Oliver Goldsmith, Historian

The business world is becoming increasingly complex and sophisticated. Consequently, entrepreneurs need various kinds of outside, professional help throughout the course of their firm's growth and development.

Q. It's pretty clear that I need some additional professional help—legal, accounting, general consulting—for my growing business. How do I go about finding the right people for these assignments? The Yellow Pages are full of names.

A. You've already taken one of the most important steps. Recognizing the need for professional assistance will ensure that the right kinds of advice and inputs are working for you before you go too far in the wrong direction.

However, picking the right advisors isn't a "slam dunk." Get ready to spend some time listing the types of assistance you need and then rigorously interviewing the various professionals who will come forth to help. Don't hesitate to grill each of the candidates as to their competencies, experience, and style of operating. Ask to see their sheepskins to guarantee that they have the requisite professional credentials. Get a list of their past clients and contact them for references. Make sure they have the specific kinds of experience that are relevant to your business and needs. Remember, "experience is the best teacher." And specialized experience is best of all.

You don't want to wind up with a "jack of all trades; master of none." For example, a good real estate attorney isn't necessarily an expert at contract law. Some are, but make sure you check out any claims to triple-decker talent. Also, make sure that you and the professionals you hire are compatible. You'll have a personal as well as a professional relationship, and these links will probably have to endure some tough, stressful times.

Here are some **Brass Tacks Tips** on retaining a good advisor:

- Get one who is willing to work to get to know you and your business.

- Find one who is willing to accept a finite assignment in the beginning. You can always expand the arrangement and make it more permanent when you are satisfied with his or her approach.

- Make sure he will be available when you need him.

- Be neither his biggest nor most complex client, nor his smallest.

- Be sure he will be able to deal well with your other advisors.

- Make sure you trust your advisor; he must be willing to tell you the unvarnished truth under any circumstance.

- Consider only people to whom you are not related.

- Once you've got a compatible, compassionate helper on board, use him. My ol' uncle Ollie used to warn: "Good advice costs the most when you don't take it."

There are a few additional **Brass Tacks Tips** that apply specifically to general business consulting assistance.

- Find advisors who function as counselors instead of consultants. Consultants generally tell you what to do. Counselors, on the other hand, help *you* figure out your best course of action. The former specializes in providing strong recommendations for specific, concrete courses of action and won't seek a lot of participation on your part. Counselors try to tap your experiences, feelings, biases and desires. They seek your active involvement in the entire process.

- Make sure that the advisor you retain has had experience as a consultant in addition to having a track record in the field of concern to your company. Given the cutbacks in industry, there are more people seeking to make a living through consulting than ever before. But knowing something and being able to convey it to you in a meaningful way are two different things. Ask for references and check them out. Don't be afraid to interview your prospects and to ask them hard questions. Use the same set of questions for all candidates.

- Describe the limits of your proposed assignment up front. Don't give the impression that yours will be an open-ended relationship or that the consultant being interviewed is the only helper you'll rely on. Let him know what you expect as outcomes and how much you are willing to pay to attain them.

- Try to avoid being anyone's largest customer. Some consultants tend to spend a lot time "learning" from their big clients. Remember, you're the one paying for help. On the flip side, the smallest clients tend to get short shrift when the "biggies" summon for aid. Get a list of any prospective advisor's other clients and a commitment that he—and not an assistant—will be available when you need him.

- Retain only candid, compassionate helpers. You want someone who'll tell you the unvarnished truth but will do it in a way that is sensitive to your hang-ups and insecurities. This is going to be one of your most important professional and personal relationships, so make sure you really like and admire the guy and that you can easily understand him. You don't need a theorist who is fluent in mumbo-jumbo and facile with two-dollar words. (This probably will exclude a lot of university professors.)

- Make sure that you—and all the employees and family members who will be involved in the project—trust the advisor. If you don't trust your source of advice you probably won't act on it. You can waste a lot of time and money getting "second opinions." Of course, make sure you give your consultant all the facts and that all of your advisors are given the same facts.

- Be sure that the consultant you select is willing to make hard-nosed judgments and stick by them. This does not mean that he will produce only one course of recommended action....and that "you *vil* like it." Good advisors give you options.

- Be confident that the counselor you select will take the initiative to get together with any other advisors you retain and that it will not be your job to get them around the same table together when joint effort is called for. You don't want to wind up "carrying the water" for a bunch of prima donnas who are "too busy" to get together. It's a good idea to assemble all of your advisors for a rump session a couple of times every year. But have a tight agenda; you'll be paying all of them by the hour.

ABOUT THE AUTHOR

Paul Willax is an experienced, award-winning journalist who has "walked the walk" in businesses both large and small. Chairman of the Center for Business Ownership Inc. based in Buffalo, New York, he is an experienced entrepreneur, business owner, corporate executive, and educator. During the past thirty-five years, Professor Willax has mixed wit with wisdom in thousands of articles, columns and presentations for business owners and managers around the world. As an award-winning newspaper and broadcast journalist, a Distinguished Professor of Entrepreneurship, and a seasoned radio and television personality, he knows how to turn on and inspire his audiences with need-to-know information and immediately-actionable advice.

He's *"gone for the gold"* in everything he's done, advancing from bank teller to CEO of a $13 billion bank voted one of the "most innovative in the world,"......from owner of the 75-year old Kazoo Co.—a family business with less than $1 million in sales—to founder of a company that grew from scratch to over $32 billion in sales......from teaching assistant to Professor of Management......from student reporter to newspaper owner and award-winning, nationally-syndicated journalist......from ham radio operator to prize-winning broadcast reporter......from door-to-door salesman to top man in over two dozen successful corporations......from PFC to Brigadier General in the military.

Dr. Willax has owned and operated successful businesses in a wide variety of industries, including retail, automotive, publishing, broadcasting, computer technology, real estate, securities brokerage, banking, insurance and audio and video production. He has both the ability and experience to help entrepreneurs, business owners and managers lead their enterprises into the third millennium. In recent years, he has concentrated on the unique issues confronting technology start-ups, rapidly-growing enterprises and businesses in crisis.

Paul Willax can be reached at the Center for Business Ownership Inc., Box 67, Clarence NY 14031 or via e mail at Willax@The-BrassTacks.com.

0-595-21792-3